CHAPTER 3

Decoding The Analytical Apple
The Thinking Spirit

The Analytical Apple Spirit

Analyzing their worlds with very crisp thought,
Competition is what they have been taught,
Being the best and knowing they are right,
Is what ignites the Apple spirit's light.

Logic and reason are their precision tools,
How well they fit into America's schools,
Serious thinking about all that they do,
Planning the future with something brand new!

Apple Spirit Comparison Worksheet

If you are an Apple spirit you…

Feel best when you are…	being productive and efficient
Feel the most reward…	when you are precisely correct and are acknowledged by others as such
Feel most at ease…	with other logical and rational people
May be seduced by…	feeling oriented people who arouse your curiosity
Avoid…	strong emotional sharing
Lead by…	objective, impersonal decision-making
Follow others who are…	clear, concise, and data-based
Enjoy activities…	that require mental challenge
Cannot understand…	people who are impulsive
Distance yourself from…	highly emotive people and events
Find your best friends in…	other Apples and thinkers
Most want a mate…	to respect you and your point of view as being correct
Feel the most pain…	when you are not understood as being fair and objective
Make the best decisions…	based on logical impersonal analysis of the data
Make the worst decisions…	when pressured for time and are unable to fully plan
Think that you are…	right and others should just accept that as fact
Need to have at all times…	the latest laptop computer and other up-to-date technology
Know your best relationship gift is…	being precise and objective

39

Spirit/Fruit Link

Providing a striking contrast to the feeling "Passionate Plum," the "Analytical Apple" is the spirit of reason and rational thought. Ripe apples off the tree are best when they are crunchy and crisp and full of vibrant flavor. In much the same way, a ripe Apple spirit can efficiently "crunch" data with the best of spirits and always has a "crisp" logical set of reasons to support their decisions. Also, just as the apple is often associated with the "American way" as reflected by the phrase "it's as American as apple pie," so too has this spirit type permeated the fabric of our society. An apple is the fruit children give to their beloved teachers; it is the fruit of the tree of knowledge; and even one of America's most famous cities has the nickname "the Big Apple." Additionally, the apple has become so intimately connected with logical efficient processing of knowledge that one of the major computer companies has used this fruit as its logo that is now recognized worldwide for its customer friendly and efficient computers. It might be quite accurate to say that we live in a society dominated by the apple's influence. Great value is placed on the intelligence and rational skills of Apple spirits who are at the core of the development of the scientific and high technology industries of the American culture. Thus, the apple with a firm skin, wonderful flavor, crispness of texture, and abundance of availability is the perfect fruit to link to this spirit type.

Apple DNA (Distinct Notable Attributes)

• *Detailed plans and mental maps*

Using clearly defined thinking strategies to form mental maps, the Apple spirit navigates through life in an objective way balancing out the costs and benefits to its every decision. Apples are easy to recognize because they are frequently heard telling others to plan for retirement, to prepare a budget, to put their lives in order, or to invest in the future. Much security and a sense of contentment are derived from the detailed plans, agendas, and itineraries that the Apple spirit creates and follows. Even when apparently relaxing, Apples are likely to be in the midst of thinking or planning something for the future. The pressure to always have detailed plans and meticulous steps enumerated to carry out those plans may make Apple spirits seem to have tunnel vision, be inflexible, and appear over-controlling to other spirits. But for the Apple, it is this attention to detail that helps them ripen and thus, leads to the successful accomplishment of its perpetual list of goals.

- *Structured environments*

Apples need a well-organized and systematic environment in which to function effectively. At work their offices will be efficiently set up to maximize productivity, their desks are likely to be neatly ordered, and their daily planners will always be close to them. At home, you can recognize an Apple spirit by their organized closets, their highly structured routines, and even their unbelievably clean garages. Compulsive neatness and order give the Apple spirit per-ceived control over what they often find to be a chaotic world. Apples thrive and are energized when making order in their lives out of per-ceived chaos.

- *Consistent linear thinking and behavior*

Apple spirits strive for continuity and consistency in their lives, feeling compelled to behave in a manner that fits these principles. They run their lives on regular predictable routines because this is what is most efficient and effective in helping them reach their goals. Apples may seem stubborn and impatient to other spirit types when unanticipated factors make demands on their time or when any irregularity upsets the flow of their plans. For example, Apples may know exactly at what moment a particular traffic light will be green and heaven help a slow Plum driver that might cause an Apple to miss the green light and be thrown off its usual schedule. The Apple spirit simply demands consistency in all aspects of its life to maximize energy flow and to ensure an optimal ripening environment.

- *Impersonal non-emotional expression*

Apple spirits do not pick up readily on emotional cues from others and can be counted upon to respond to most events in their lives in an impersonal, non-emotional manner. This detachment from emotion allows them to objectively evaluate circumstances independent of the specific people involved. Other spirit types may view the Apple as being cold, detached, uncaring, and lacking in spontaneity and enthusiasm, but for the Apple, objectivity must be maintained in order to ensure valid and reliable assessment. Unlike the passionate Plum spirit that emotes loudly and frequently, the Apple will avoid public emotional displays at all costs and will deal with its feelings by thinking itself through a situation, rather than feeling itself through. At the end of this thought process, the Apple will always do the right thing.

Apple Spirit Language: Thoughts

Whereas the language of the Plum spirit was feelings, the Apple spirit communicates with the world through its thoughts. The Apple spirit is energized in environments in which it can fully utilize its capacity for precise logical thought and analytical reasoning and successfully communicate that to others. Apples know that no other spirit types are as competent as they are at thinking their way through problems and decisions and arriving at the best solution. Sherlock Holmes's famous quote, "It's elementary, my Dear Watson..." echoes the efficiency and pride of the Apple's deductive reasoning process. When faced with decisions, the Apple uses well-defined, systematic, and logical processes to literally interface its mind with the pertinent details and facts it observes. It then rearranges and organizes the facts into a clear, orderly form for careful analysis. This meticulous thought process ensures the Apple spirit will arrive at the logical and best course of action. Few other spirits care to go to such lengths in making decisions. Few other spirits are quite as precise as the Apple. And no other spirit communicates with the world in such a purely objective analytical way. You are well on your way to recognizing an Apple spirit when you hear them give their favorite piece of advice "think about it thoroughly before you act."

Primary Apple Need: To be Right

The Apple spirit is energized through thoughtfully solving challenging problems, doing the correct thing at the correct time, and leading others through the maze of life with crisp, precise, unemotional leadership. Underlying all of these activities is its core need: to be right. Being the best thinker of all spirit types and driven by a need to utilize its intellectual prowess, the Apple spirit will seek opportunities to competitively pit wits, discuss, debate, or dispute in order to show the perfection of its logic and reasoning abilities. It thrives on intellectual competition so it can meet its need to be right. Even very good reasoning offered by a different type spirit can be skillfully reprocessed by the Apple spirit in such a way that the Apple's logic may ultimately appear most correct. Most frustrating to other intelligent spirits is that, when presented with excellent logic, the Apple can mentally maneuver itself into the position of being in perfect agreement, but for more precise reasons. Other spirits may view this process as being one-upmanship, but Apples will not see it that way. The Apple simply is being absolutely correct for the correct reasons.

Well-ordered words delivered in a deliberate and measured manner, unencumbered or confused by emotion make the Apple very effective in communicating the correctness of its facts and information. Unlike the Plum spirit who is swept away by its feelings and often speaks from the realms of the philosophical, hypothetical, and abstract, the Apple spirit, with its detached observer frame of reference, views the world more objectively. It reads the black and white lines of reality rather than speculating on and interpreting all the shades of gray that lie between them. The Apple needs to be right and will not be distracted from that goal by any less rational approach.

Decoding Apple Relationships
Family, Friends, and Acquaintances

• *Costs/benefits analysis*

The Apple spirit can make a most interesting and often very stimulating friend or partner. However, the Apple is usually methodical in forming relationships. Never will an Apple make a permanent commitment to another person until it has had sufficient time to analyze all the pragmatic advantages of such a commitment for itself and for the other person. This cost/benefit analysis is simply a practical way of finding qualified partners to meet its needs. The Apple wants to ensure that the friend or partner lives up to the Apple's standards and will neatly fit into the appropriate compartment of its life. However, once an Apple spirit makes a commitment, it will be a dedicated, loyal, and practical friend or partner and will provide abundant safety, security, and consistency for those it values.

• *Information-centered conversations*

In conversations with other spirits the Apple's approach will be information centered. If it sees that a person has something important to offer, the Apple spirit will give that person undivided attention. However, if the content of the discussion is emotionally based, perceived as irrelevant, or a load of unsubstantiated opinion, the Apple may just as likely tune that person out. The Apple is not being mean-spirited; it just desires a different type of stimulation.

In the event that another spirit should find itself in a situation in which it must converse with an Apple that it does not know, it is best not to ask the Apple questions such as, "How do you *feel* about…?" Rather, simply ask the Apple, "What do you think about…?" or say

"I have never quite understood the..." When given the conversational lead, the Apple will take it gladly and the other spirit may just sit back, listen, and learn.

- *Teaching/mentoring relationships with friends*

Apples love to teach and explain. All that is required of another spirit type is to keep the conversation flowing with the Apple by asking intelligent questions, requesting clarification, and complimenting the Apple on its ideas. By listening to what the Apple has to say, other spirits can learn a lot about the Apple's interests, and indirectly about its likes and dislikes. Other thinking spirits may wish to engage in a more balanced discussion, but unless you are another Apple, be prepared to let the Apple's ideas and logic take the lead and keep it.

- *Orderly and predictable love life*

Working hard to direct their lives in an orderly and predictable course, Apple spirits will offer few surprises and little spontaneity. The more spontaneous spirits may find themselves the constant target of the Apple's favorite question, "Why?" Woe is it to the unprepared spirit who responds with some other less thought-out reason because the Apple will be quick to reveal the flaws in another's judgment or logic even if that person is the Apple's most cherished person. Unless the Apple's frustration to comprehend illogical behavior is understood, other spirit types may feel the sting of what they may believe to be the Apple's condescending attitude toward unqualified actions or emotionally based rationale. But in reality-the Apple is just being an "Analytical Apple."

Romantic Love Relationships

- *Planned romantic perfection*

In relating on a romantic level to the Apple, other spirits must understand and learn to read Apple behavior. For example, when an

Apple plans an important date, its feelings for the partner may be translated into creating advanced detailed plans and its painstaking efforts to ensure no inconveniences or surprises are encountered. On the date the Apple may make a more feeling spirit feel as if he/she is being wined and dined by a business executive who is scrutinizing another company before a major merger. Apples will make every attempt to make other spirits feel valued by the length they go to in making plans, spending money, and making everything perfect on the date.

- *Love is only one spoke in the wheel of the Apple's life*

For Apples, attachments to others and to life do not derive from any single event or person, but rather to the whole-integrated system of which the individual or event is merely one strand. Once woven in, however, each strand is an essential part of the overall design. Life for an Apple is like a wheel that has many spokes. Relationships are merely one spoke on their wheel with other equally important spokes being its career, friends, hobbies, investments, etc. Each spoke on the wheel provides the Apple spirit with essential energy. In romantic relationships with Apples, other spirit types must realize that sometimes they will be all important (when their spoke comes up for attention) and at other times they may be completely ignored depending on the Apple's other priorities of the moment. At these times family and friends can avoid feeling abandoned by helping the Apple with its current goal (spoke). Though the Apple spirit is not likely to admit such sentiment, it will be pleased to feel the support and cooperation from others whom it now believes have the same "right" priorities.

- *Gifts as an expression of sentiment*

Though Apples tend to be more rational than emotional, that is not to say that they do not have feelings. Their feelings, such as affection, will be shown, but only in a logical way and at a time when it is practical to do so. Apples usually express romantic love for others in material ways. It just makes more sense to the Apple to translate feelings into the price tag on a gift. For example, the bigger the diamond ring, the more the love. Of course the Apple likes to receive its love in the same manner. Plums should be warned that letters expressing tender sentiment, love poems, and blossoms picked along a woodland path might receive an "Oh, how nice!" but not move the Apple to ask for a second date. But invite the Apple over to dinner, have an expensive bottle of wine, followed by a challenging game of chess, and a then a congenial discussion about the stock market or the latest computer technology, and you will impress the Apple all the way to its core.

When the Code Goes Wrong: Obstacles to Growth and Ripening

Apples are the spirit type that relate to the world primarily through thinking and whose number one need is to be right. Because of their predominant reliance on linear thinking and also their natural resistance to accept other forms of processing reality as being valid, Apples often encounter problems when circumstances or different spirit types require non-linear feeling responses. When forced from their comfortable analytical processing zone, Apples will struggle to relate to others positively and may become quite stressed which never brings out the best in the Apple.

- *Difficulty handling emotions*

Apples are not adept at negotiating what they perceive as the irrationality and inconsistency of feelings and may come across harsh or insensitive. Apples are the first spirit to hand an emotionally upset person a tissue so that person can stop crying and become less emotional. Unlike intuitive Plums that use their feelings to make decisions that are more compatible with their internal subjective reality and believe that feelings are strengths, emotional feelings cause static and interference in the Apples' efforts to see a clear and objective picture of reality. Feelings for Apples are definitely viewed as a weakness. Apples must perceive reality through clearly inputting information from the outside world into their internal mental processor for analysis. This input process must be kept static free to permit valid and reliable analysis. Thus, while it is best for Apples to make their major life decisions based on thoughts rather than feelings, when relating with other more feeling oriented spirits or being in emotionally charged situations, Apples need to learn to validate and acknowledge the value of emotions for others. Then they need to integrate this assessment into their thinking and decision-making processes so that others will better be able to receive the practical assistance that Apples are offering.

- *"Tunnel vision"*

We live in an Apple society, one in which people are rewarded for good thinking, making correct choices, and living in a predictable structured ways. We are rewarded for conforming to standards, being on time, having a work ethic, setting goals and priorities, and planning for the future. This Apple philosophy so deeply permeates our society that Apples living and working in such a comfortable environment may lose awareness of or even become unwilling to acknowledge that the world is comprised of many different spirit types each having their own truths and ways of knowing. If this occurs, the Apple spirit may become rigid, narrow-minded, and dogmatic. Knowing that the logical approach has worked flawlessly in its own life, the Apple may impose its highly structured and ordered lifestyle on other spirit types for whom it is not appropriate. With this tunnel vision, Apples may demand that others follow their procedures, timetables, and adopt their goals and standards. Rigid Apples can make more sensitive spirit-friends and family members feel like only one more possession acquired in the Apple's string of successes. Over-ripe Apples may become so driven by the need to logically analyze anything and everything, that they irritate other spirits with their demeanor. Apples do need to analyze information, but must always remember that their way is not everyone else's way. In relationships, Apples need to "offer" advice when asked for it and to learn to "prefer" that others will take that advice, but not "demand" that they use this advice if it does not fit.

• *Stress*

If not careful, the Apple spirit can become obsessed with the cleverness of its own logic. Its need for perfection may become an obsession and since perfection is rarely obtained the Apple may create its own stress and be prone to fits of anger from the frustration of not achieving perfection. These self-defeating behaviors are most likely to occur when its goals or those it has for others are not achieved or are not achieved on the Apple's pre-planned schedule. Unripe Apples may suffer stress from a lack of precision causing them to have to work longer hours in order to achieve important goals. They may become so tuned out in their quest for success that they fall prey to becoming workaholics and thereby limit other potentially energy-producing people and activities on their wheel of life. Often it may take a personal crisis such as a heart attack or divorce to remind these driven Apple spirits about the consequences of neglecting the rest of their wheel of life. However, Apples can recover from these crises and obstacles to achieve a more balanced and meaningful life if they make the necessary changes and move to a more balanced perspective that actually is the "right" thing to do.

Another source of stress occurs when the Apple finds itself at odds with other spirit types that do not concede to the Apple the prize of being right. When not recognized for being the best or rewarded for work well done, the Apple may react by brooding, becoming irritable, or being more task-oriented than usual. Apples that have not been recognized for their achievements over time (overripe fruit) may become sour, negative, depressed, and argumentative, looking for every opportunity to score a point and earning them the reputation of being stubborn, opinionated, and every bit a "Scrooge." Apples need to learn to self-monitor their own behaviors and process success inwardly, so they do not depend on others entirely for feedback about their many successes.

Putting It All Together: The Apple Spirit

When the Apple spirit is fully actualized it will yield its fruit of "virtuous knowledge" to the world. Not only is this knowledge of the type that will advance people's wellbeing such as medical and technological advancements, but also the Apple's gifts can actually help the moral fiber of the world by serving as a conscience for what is "right" and what is "wrong." When Apple spirits ripen, they are among the most righteous of all people. Great thinking Apple leaders such as Abraham Lincoln, Winston Churchill, and Eleanor Roosevelt, frontier forging scientists like Albert Einstein, Madam Curie, and Jonas Salk, and driven inventors like Henry Ford and Thomas Edison have bettered the world. Of course we cannot forget Steve Jobs, CEO and co-founder of Apple Inc. whose work has brought the precision of the Apple spirit into so many lives with his company's cutting edge products and services. The Apple spirit shines in books like H. G. Wells's *The Time Machine* or in movies/television shows like *Star Trek* with the pure Apple characters of Mr. Spock and Lieutenant Commander Data. Thus, when ripe, the analytical Apple will use its knowledge for the good of all, whether it is for their family and friends, or for all of humanity. The Apple spirit is all about thinking and knowledge and has led to some of the most incredible scientific, theoretical, and technological advances in history.

APPLE CODE SUMMARY

Distinct Notable Attributes	Logical analysis of information
	Systematic, planned, and
	orderly decision-making
	Future orientation in planning goals
	Detailed plans and schedules
	Recognized for doing
	precisely the "right" thing
	Linear, impersonal expression
Spirit Language	Thoughts
Core Spirit Needs	To be right
	To have a predictable lifestyle
	based on logic and reason
	To be challenged by new
	frontiers of knowledge
	To ask "Why?" and
	then "Why not?"
Relationships	Analyzes the cost/benefit
	ratio of its relationships
	Relationships are just one of many
	spokes on their wheel of life
	To connect to other minds
	through reason and logic
Obstacles to Growth	May suffer stress related problems
	Have difficulties relating
	effectively to emotions
	May inappropriately impose its
	structured lifestyle on others
Gift of the Spirit	Virtuous knowledge

Now that you can identify Apples and Plums, please read the next chapter; to decode the Pineapple spirit.

CHAPTER 4

Decoding The Pleasing Pineapple
The Dual-Modality Spirit

The Pleasing Pineapple Spirit

Able to relate to all fruits fine;
Wanting to please is its unique sign.
Using both Apple thoughts and Plum feelings,
The Pineapple is really quite appealing.

Deciding just what it wants to do,
May often put it in quite a stew.
Deliberate and prudent in all ways,
To win its approval, just give it praise.

The Pineapple Spirit Comparison Worksheet

If you are a Pineapple spirit you…

Feel best when you are…	pleasing to others and are productive
Feel the most reward…	when you provide practical service to others
Feel most at ease…	with any type of "ripe" fruit
May be seduced by…	others giving you approval but not being sincere
Lead by…	mutual exchange of communication
Follow others who are…	practical, reliable, and consistent
Enjoy activities that…	move both your feelings and your thoughts
Cannot understand…	people who are prejudiced or biased
Distance yourself from…	people who are pessimistic and negative
Find your best friends in…	other Pineapples
Most want a mate to…	to appreciate both your mind and heart
Feel the most pain…	when having to decide among many alternatives
Make the best decisions…	based on a balance between your mind and heart
Make the worst decisions…	when pressured for time
Think that you are…	a pretty good teacher
Need to have at all times…	others to connect with
Know your best relationship gift is…	getting along with lots of diverse types of spirits

Spirit/Fruit Link

Having both a "p" for plum and also the word "apple" in its name, the pineapple is the perfect fruit to represent the next spirit type. On a continuum, with the feeling Plum at one extreme and the thinking Apple at the other end, the nature of the Pineapple spirit falls midway between, for it represents a perfect blended union between thought and feeling. The pineapple was chosen to represent this spirit type because it is the fruit most commonly used to blend together different fruits and flavors in a fruit salad. Likewise, the Pineapple's duality of expression equips it with the unique abilities to blend well with and successfully bring together diverse types of people.

At first glance, the pineapple fruit may appear a little off-putting with its pinecone textured surface and its spiny-edged leaf top, but cut a ripe one open and you are rewarded with a delightful, sweet tasty surprise. In like manner, the Pineapple spirit's natural intelligence, casual aloofness, and industriousness may at first seem a little prickly or intimidating; however, once understood at a deeper level, they can be appreciated for their joyful enthusiasm, powerful down-to-earth common sense, and overflowing compassion toward others.

If you saw traits of yourself or others in both the Plum spirit and the Apple spirit, it is very likely that you and/or they have a Pineapple spirit!

Pineapple DNA (Distinct Notable Attributes)

- *Dual-modality*

The "dual-modality" of being able to move seamlessly between its thoughts and feelings defines the Pineapple spirit. Like Plums, the Pineapple spirit is sensitive to feelings, but is not dominated by those feelings. It can "think past them" in order to put those emotions in perspective and to their most appropriate use. The Pineapple will always take time to genuinely empathize with the feelings of

others, but then go further in being able to offer insight and practical advice. Likewise, the Pineapple spirit can competently participate when logical and analytical thinking is taking place, though
the Pineapple's thinking is not quite as precise as that of the Apple;
nor does it have the over-riding need to be right. The Pineapple can
temper the purely rational and objective by reframing it with a bit of
personal and subjective softening. Overall, the Pineapple can experience feelings much more deeply and successfully than the Apple, but
not as deeply as the Plum; and while its thinking is more logical and
linear than the Plum, it is not as precisely logical as the Apple.

- *Unpredictability*

The ability of Pineapple spirits to move effortlessly, seamlessly,
and spontaneously between their thinking and feeling modes may
give them the appearance of being unpredictable. When thoughts
trigger feelings or feelings trigger thoughts, the Pineapple may suddenly shift modes, baffling others around them. They may appear to
be devil-may-care, spontaneous, and uninhibited in one instant, and
then suddenly something triggers a switch, and the next moment
they will be caught up in their thoughts, becoming quiet, pensive,
or appear brooding. You may go out to lunch with a "Plum," but
return to work with an "Apple" after the Pineapple gets the bill. The
Pineapple that scrupulously shops for sales and buys nothing without a coupon may suddenly blow the whole cookie jar on something frivolous. A word of caution: don't try to predict which way the
Pineapple will go! Just enjoy the ride and realize that the Pineapple is
just being a Pineapple.

- *Struggles with decision-making*

One of the most distinguishing characteristics of the Pineapple
spirit is the trouble it has making decisions, particularly when the
needs, desires, or preferences of others come into play. In fact, when a
decision involves another valued person, the Pineapple may become

completely immobilized without adequate input from that person. When forced to act or decide without information from the other, the Pineapple will labor greatly in making a decision, and later feel it necessary to provide copious rationale to support its decision. If not met with approval, the Pineapple may then change its mind, or be readily persuaded to see another point-of-view. This is not to say that Pineapples are "wishy-washy"; they are highly flexible when options are equitable, or when the other person is held in high-esteem. They can, however, stand firm on issues that prompt their heart or mind to do so.

You will often recognize a Pineapple when you overhear frequent remarks about feeling one way, but thinking another, or vice versa. For example, "I feel like painting the house yellow, but I think the neighbors might object." A Pineapple might want to give another spirit a big hug, but at the same moment, its brain will be rapidly processing whether or not this is the right thing to do in this place at this time with this person.

Pineapples may appear indecisive about the smallest things. One might struggle to get a prompt and straight forward answer from a Pineapple when asking where it might like to go to dinner or what movie it might like to see. Common Pineapple responses will be, "Oh, I don't care. Where do you want to go?" or "Anything is OK with me." To the more decisive spirits, this characteristic can be maddening for they feel they can never really know the Pineapple's true likes and preferences when in reality the Pineapple is just being its "pleasing" self.

• *Highly effective communication skills*

Pineapples are highly effective communicators because they are excellent listeners and "read" both the content and emotional tone when in conversation with others. Being able to hear both the words and intuit deeper meaning from body language, they are well equipped to respond effectively. Their sincere desire to find out about another may lead to intense probing questions that may make others, particularly Apples, a bit uneasy. Excellent skills at perception and communication enable them to be keenly insightful, intuitive, and skilled at assessing human behavior. They are thus, well equipped to render a high quality of meaningful interaction and provide sound counsel.

- *Adept at bringing harmony to diverse groups*

Because of their wide acceptance of people, beliefs, and points-of-view, Pineapples can prevent lines of communication from becoming blocked between people, as they sometimes must do with the more strongly opinionated types. Pineapple spirits are extremely diplomatic. When individuals are too highly emotional or, in the other extreme, too coldly rational, Pineapples can help guide the tenor back toward balance. For example, they can personalize an impersonal business exchange, or they can help focus and ground an individual whose feelings are escalating. Pineapples can help parties in conflict mediate and negotiate areas of conflict by refocusing their attention on positive and shared interests. Finally, their sensitivity to others allows Pineapple spirits to effectively engage in meaningful exchanges with diverse spirit types who may be quite different in their styles of communication.

Pineapple Spirit Language: A Duality of Thoughts and Feelings

The Pineapple uses a dual-modality to communicate with the world: its core SELF speaks easily using a combination of thoughts and feelings, and it becomes ripe and actualized through this duality of experience. A thriving Pineapple spirit may choose to work in a job that challenges its thinking skills, but then finds activities or relationships outside work that allow for the expression of its emotional side. Most importantly, the energy that the Pineapple spirit needs to ripen—to become the full expression of their full human potential—comes from having roots deeply planted in the fertile soil of their emotional and intellectual life and from basking in the rich, warm sunshine of an environment in which they can express both feelings and thoughts and be embraced by others who understand and appreciate them.

Primary Pineapple Need: To Please and Gain Approval

The Pineapple might be described as the "pleasing" spirit. If you are a Pineapple, your primary need is not just for love, like the Plum; nor is it to be right, like the Apple. To gain the approval of others is the primary need of the Pineapple spirit. Pineapples become highly energized when such responses are forthcoming. They thrive best in the sunshine of positive affirmations and validation for their decisions, actions, and quality of being.

Decoding Pineapple Relationships
Family, Friends, and Acquaintances

• *Seek low stress relationships balanced by emotion and thought*

Pineapples thrive in an environment where they can maintain many long-time, steady, moderate-intensity relationships with family, friends, and acquaintances. They seek balance in all relationship states without high tension and stress. They will use rational thought to work through their more intense emotions, often resulting in the need for a good debate-type argument when in a situation of conflict. And when thoughts hammer relentlessly in the Pineapple mind over issues that cannot be laid to rest, the Pineapple may respond by exhibiting high levels of emotional intensity. For example, a Pineapple at the breaking point from too much thinking may suddenly start laughing over something to the point of near incapacitation!

Pineapples will push, endure, and pressure themselves; stretch far and endure much in order to receive positive attention from others in the form of compliments, praise, acts of service, or other tokens of approval. Such gifts to their spirit will spark and ignite the Pineapple spirit to full actualization.

- *Accepting and non-judgmental*

More accepting of the differences between people than most of the other spirit types, they mix well with a variety of spirits. As a matter-of-fact, such things as a person's gender, race, or status may hardly register with the Pineapple; they tune into the person rather than to that person's particular traits. You can expect most Pineapples to be accepting, non-judgmental, and most of all positive and dependable supporters. And they naturally attract a widely diverse group of spirits into their circle of friends.

- *Congenial*

The Pineapple is a friendly spirit. They are easy to be around and thrive on amicable relationships that are low in conflict and tension. Other spirits describe them as generous, pleasant, agreeable, responsive, and charming. When they receive positive acknowledgement and feel accepted, Pineapple spirits will brighten the lives around them with their unconditional positive regard, enthusiasm, genuine interest, hard work, and unselfish natures.

- *Reliable and dependable*

Because they are highly practical and possess a good degree of common sense, Pineapples can be depended on to help solve the problems of daily life. They can efficiently organize a jumble of facts into a meaningful whole, or produce sensible and useful ideas to clarify a confused situation. They are dependable and reliable because it just doesn't make sense to be otherwise. Organized at work and at home, they are often seen with lists, agendas, and appointment books. Although, it is not unusual for them to misplace them, calendars and sticky notes adorn their workspace. Pineapples are prompt and efficient in meeting their responsibilities and are conscientious in keeping their word and in meeting the expectations of others.

- *Wide range of interests*

Pineapples gravitate toward the novel and unique; they are end-lessly delighted with the big canvas upon which life is painted. When a Pineapple says that they do not really have a preference when a choice is offered, this may be the honest truth. These multifaceted people have a wide variety of interests and are open to all kinds of experiences, save for a few of the more-risky adventures taken by their Orange friends. They have a great capacity to enjoy and appre-ciate a wide variety of music, art, literature, food, and entertainment. In a single week, their movie interests may include a heart-rending tragedy, a ridiculous comedy, a high-suspense thriller (No horror, please!) or a tender romance. They can be mesmerized by a classical ballet; savor jazz in a funky, offbeat nightclub; or hang out at the neighborhood pub after work. They can enjoy a strenuous hike on a grubby camping trip, or lounging on the deck of a cruise ship. You might find them shopping in an elegant boutique, or mucking out an animal pen. You are likely to see Pineapples perusing books in almost every section of the bookstore. They are a truly delicious multifaceted spirit that brings different spirits together.

- *Fun-loving*

Pineapples delight in play and have an almost childlike enthusi-asm. They love exploring anything new. From childhood through the gray and balding stage, you will find them boarding roller coasters and haunting assorted amusement theme parks. It can take them hours to walk a stretch of beach as they sift through shell fragments, reams of seaweed, and smelly debris washed in by the tide. Even if unaccustomed to rigorous exercise, they will hike long and tire-lessly through a new terrain. They like to get together with friends for game nights. They love decorating the house, yard and mailbox for holidays. They are the spirits that are least likely to complain of boredom, as they can find something of interest almost anywhere.

Romantic Love Relationships

• *Balance of intimacy and commitment*

With a balance of intimacy and commitment, Pineapple spirits make excellent partners for romantic relationships with a variety of spirit types. Not as love-focused and passionate as the Plum, nor tending to compartmentalize love and romance like the Apple, the Pineapple makes love connections that tend to balance the two extremes. That is not to say that a Pineapple spirit cannot swing into a passionate mood, or that they cannot put their romantic feelings "on hold" while they focus on other things. But they are more likely to mix the ambience of a candlelight dinner with thought-provoking and stimulating conversation. They can also pull this together beautifully on the spur-of-the moment without a lot of planning.

• *Responds to intelligent sincerity*

Since finding love is not an overarching need, Pineapples tend to be more cautious and to fall in love slowly. They are not likely to let their feelings of infatuation run away with them, as their good practical sense will keep those feelings under reign. You are not likely to meet a Pineapple at a single's bar for a "one night stand." Ripe Pineapples will see right through a "come-on" line; they respond to intelligent sincerity. They tend to fall in love with classmates, workmates, or long-term friends with whom they have had repetitive, sustained contact.

• *Highly attuned to partner's needs*

Pineapples make great love companions. Their desire to please makes them highly in tune to their significant others and able to connect on emotional, physical, and intellectual fronts. They are dedicated partners. The pattern of emotional highs-and-lows when falling in-and-out of love over and over does not sit well with them.

Neither do they possess the strong opinions, beliefs, or expectations that often cause relationship disruption. Once committed, one can expect a steady, easy-going, long-term relationship with a Pineapple spirit.

- *Need a partner that will help them stay balanced*

Pineapple partners need to be aware that for the Pineapple to exist for too long in either their thinking or feeling mode will result in tension and stress. As a result, they may become irritable, unpredictable, erratic, withdrawn, or apathetic. Such behaviors should not be taken personally, will pass quickly, and do not indicate disinterest or a loss of intimacy. The Pineapple is simply in a temporary state of exhaustion. If your Pineapple partner is worn down from too much thinking or feeling, take them to an amusement park or out to play miniature golf! Let them have fun for a while! Above all, remember that the Pineapple spirit thrives on pleasing others and gaining their approval. They "do" for others to see pleasure and excitement in their faces, or to hear words of appreciation and approval. Give them plenty of sincere compliments, positive attention to their work, and "do" back for them. This is the validation they most seek, and it is the spark that ignites and fully actualizes their spirits.

When the Code Goes Wrong: Obstacles to Growth and Ripening

The Pineapple spirit meets the world through a balance of mental and emotional experience. Pineapples move toward the fully authentic expression of their spirit when their mental and emotional strengths can be effectively employed to please others and gain positive recognition and approval (their own special sunshine). But their dynamic duality, approval-seeking behavior, and hardworking nature can render them vulnerable to problems and "bruising" circumstances that have the power to diminish spirit-actualization and slow the ripening of the Pineapple spirit.

- *Trouble maintaining balance between feelings and thoughts*

While the interplay between feelings and thoughts is the distinguishing feature of the Pineapple spirit, this trait may create problems when one modality dominates for too long, or when both become intensely engaged for an extended period.

An example of a situation in which one mode exists to the exclusion of the other might occur when a Pineapple is deeply involved in a thinking task. Because of the desire to do its best work and gain praise and approval, the Pineapple spirit may block out any form of positive emotional experience that would counterbalance the intense and long hours of focused work. Mistakes may increase as thinking becomes fatigued, and frustration will build. At this point, Pineapples may react to outside stress or interruption by striking out in frustration at an available target. They may become curt with others, kick over a trashcan, or even tear up their papers in a flurry of ire. If a friend or partner has been the target, hurt, hard feelings, and shaken trust can create more tension and stress in the situation. In addition, those from whom the Pineapple hopes to receive positive acknowledgement may be far less willing to render it. Conversely, if the Pineapple is in a situation demanding too much from its emotional side, it will display signs of fatigue, stress, and tension in the form of irritability, apathy, or withdrawal. The Pineapple spirit may then seek sanctuary in a quiet and purely cognitive task. Pineapples need to remember to take breaks from too much immersion in either side of their nature.

There will also be situations that call both aspects into intense interplay, with thoughts generating intense feelings, and feelings generating excessive episodes of thinking that then generate more feelings and so on. When the emotions are positive, this cycle of intensity involving both domains leads to a high level of involvement or task-orientation, resulting in work that is very well executed, thorough, and comprehensive. However, situations in which a Pineapple regularly experiences conflict with or hostility from another spirit may cause stress to settle into their inner lives. These conditions may generate over-thinking, leading to feelings of intense anxiety, fear, guilt, or self-blame. They may think long and deeply about an event or person that has been disturbing to them, and once again, get caught up in the cycle of thinking-feeling-thinking, etc. for far longer than they should. This can lead to loss of energy and even depression. Pineapples should avoid work situations that cause a clashing of goals, ambiguity over who has what responsibility, or that result in other forms of interpersonal conflict. During times of on-going problems, they need the positive support of others. And when in relationship with those that tend to be confrontational and argumentative, they can help forestall this cycle by asking for clarification of the issue and developing assertive communication skills when discussing those issues.

- *Too much routine*

Mental and physical fatigue can result when the Pineapple is subjected to too much routine. Though other spirits may thrive in an environment that stays pretty constant from day-to-day, the Pineapple spirit needs novelty, new interests, change, and a variety of stimulating physical, emotional, and intellectual challenges. If existing too long in a static state, Pineapple spirits begin to show signs of restlessness, lose enthusiasm, and can become very dull and apathetic. Pineapples thrive in a life in which major factors are in place, such as home, significant others, and job. But within these firmly established areas, there need to be rich opportunities for stimulation, such as travel, on-going learning, new projects, and opportunities for change at work in the scope and skills used on the job or prospects of meeting more diverse spirits.

When the Pineapple lacks grounding in a solid sense of self, there is an elusiveness to them that can be disconcerting. Their interests and pursuits may seem fleeting. In addition, Pineapples can be bruised because they tend to attribute good intentions to others when this might not be so. When Pineapples have been repeatedly bruised, they may become timid in social encounters, making them appear aloof, cold, and distant. Other spirits may find it hard to "get to know" a bruised Pineapple; and bruised Pineapples may not even "get to know" themselves until well after the bruising events have occurred.

- *Can't please everyone*

Pineapples will do well to remember the adage "you can't please all the people all the time." Regardless of one's best efforts and intentions, pleasing and approval don't always happen. Instead of being "crushed" and feeling hurt or defensive when disappointed by the responses of others, Pineapple spirits need to learn that it is often not "personal," but rather that it is just another person acting according to their own nature. For example, Pineapples' extraverted friendliness is not a trait shared by some of the other spirit types. A direct confrontation or challenge to their ideas, abruptness, lapses in contact, or lack of enthusiastic response should not automatically be interpreted as signs of disapproval or lack of interest. When harsh criticism, rejection, censuring, or even indifference occurs, Pineapples can help soften the bruising that can occur when they learn that the most definitive standard for performance ultimately comes from within. Pineapples can learn that they do not always have to agree, compromise, or give in. There are other collaborative ways to manage amicably. Pineapples can strengthen themselves by simply spending time kindly with themselves and getting to know their own values, beliefs, opinions, and preferences; not to the exclusion of others, but in order to set boundaries, find their own voices, define interests, and strongly direct their own lives from the inside in order to become strong captains of their own ships.

Putting It All Together: The Pineapple Spirit

When the Pineapple spirit is fully actualized, it possesses an amazing ability to bridge differences between people through inspirational communication that can bring peace, harmony, and healing into our world. Examples of this peacemaking spirit can be seen in such political leaders as Mahatma Gandhi, Desmond Tutu, Jimmy Carter, and Barack Obama. Its teaching legacy may be found in the writings of such diverse Pineapple spirits like Helen Keller, Nelson Mandela, and Og Mandino. The spirit of Richard Bach's *Jonathon Livingston Seagull* and Mitch Albom's tribute to his teacher Morrie Schwartz in his bestselling book *Tuesdays with Morrie* resound with the powerful positive Pineapple message to live fully and learn something each day. Dynamic creations by artists like Andrew Lloyd Webber, who combined music, dance, and story to move both the mind and heart of audiences with productions like *Jesus Christ Superstar*, *Evita*, and *Phantom of the Opera*, further highlight the broad and energy producing appeal of the Pineapple spirit. The Pineapple spirit messages of tolerance, peace, and harmony may speak directly to the soul resonating from people like Martin Luther King Jr., Peter Marshall, Pope Francis, and the Dalai Lama. Perhaps, the best way to summarize the gift of the Pineapple spirit is to simply say that the ripe Pineapple spirit is the dynamic diplomatic peacemaker and bridge builder of a common communication between the different spirit types of the world.

PINEAPPLE CODE SUMMARY

Distinct Notable Attributes	Dual-modality—is able to use both thoughts and feelings
	Unpredictable; others may not predict which modality they will be in at any moment
	Practical and reliable
	Struggle in decision-making
	Highly competent communicators
Spirit Language	Duality of thoughts and feelings
Core Spirit Need	To please and gain approval from other spirit-types
Relationships	Charming and easily relates with all spirit types
	Accepting and non-judgmental of others
	Congenial and fun-loving
	A reliable and dependable friend/partner
Obstacles to Growth	Get stressed when thoughts and feelings are not balanced
	Cannot take too much routine
	May have weak personal boundaries
Gift of the Spirit	Peacemakers

And now you have the Pineapple code, read the next chapter to decode the Peaches in your life.

CHAPTER 5

Decoding The Talkative Peach
The Verbal Spirit

The Talkative Peach Spirit

Peaches most of all want to be heard,
And so they love the spoken word,
Intentions are good; advice is sound,
The Peach is forever, social bound.

Loyal and caring, the Peach is true,
Though it will worry much about you.
They are always kind and lovely to meet,
The talkative Peach is simply hard to beat.

The Peach Spirit Comparison Worksheet

If you are a Peach spirit you…

Feel best when you are…	talking with others
Feel the most reward…	when you provide helpful advice to others
Feel most at ease…	with any spirit willing to listen
May be seduced by…	controlling, in charge types of spirits
Avoid…	being alone
Lead by…	verbal communication
Follow others who are…	amiable, friendly, and courteous
Enjoy activities that are…	worthy of talking about later
Cannot understand…	people who interrupt you
Distance yourself from…	people that will not listen
Find your best friends in…	any spirits that value your conversation
Most want a mate to…	listen to your stories
Feel the most pain…	when isolated or cut off by others
Make the best decisions…	after you have talked it out
Make the worst decisions…	when rushing into situations without talking first
Think that you are…	knowledgeable about almost everything
Need to have at all times…	an audience
Know your best relationship gift is…	giving sound advice to others

Spirit/Fruit Link

As one thinks about a ripe peach, one's mind may invoke a picture of a plump, juicy, golden colored with red highlights, aromatic fruit. Your image may also include trees loaded with so much fruit that branches may bend or break. Notice that the peach has some similar attributes to another plump juicy fruit whose name also begins with the letter "P," the "Passionate Plum." All of these characteristics help will us accurately decode the Peach spirit.

Peach spirits are in many ways first cousins to Plum spirits. Like Plum spirits, Peach spirits enjoy the sunshine of being with people and focus much of their energy around feelings, although they are not as consumed by empathizing with feelings as the Plum. When golden ripe, peaches are full of sweet nectar just oozing out. Likewise, ripe Peach spirits are always full of stories and news they eagerly await to share with others. They are the extroverted feeling spirit, while the Plum is the introverted feeling spirit. Peach spirits have so much information inside (they are plump with juice) that they simply cannot wait to share. And when a perceived invitation to share is given (and even sometimes when it is not), the Peach spirit will eagerly share and share and share. The Peach receives positive feelings simply from verbally talking with people. Also, like Plum spirits, Peach spirits need to be treated tenderly because they are sensitive and can bruise easily. But, if they are provided a lot of sunshine in their immediate environment, they will certainly provide a pleasant personality for other spirits to enjoy. While Plums have been described as the spirit of the heart, Apples as the spirit of the mind, and Pineapples as spirit with a dual processor of both heart and mind, the Peach most appropriately can be described as the verbal spirit that has something to say.

Peach DNA (Distinct Notable Attributes)

- *Verbally expressive about its opinions*

Peaches are the true social interaction spirits of the world. They love interacting with people of all kinds and types and at the same time enjoy learning about all kinds of things. In fact the Peach is likely to know a little bit about many things and be quite accurate in this knowledge. Of course this knowledge allows the Peach spirit to communicate with a lot of different people about many different things. This ability equips the Peach for its favorite pastime, social interaction. Peaches love to form opinions about the many things they know a little bit about and are eager to pass these opinions on to others that they encounter.

- *Socially extroverted and outgoing (no one is a stranger to the Peach)*

Peach spirits are likely to strike up a conversation with anyone at any time. They simply love chatting. They seek out and create social gatherings of groups of people with whom they can visit, but are just at home if they only have one other person with whom to interact. If they cannot find another person to socialize with in person, they turn to their favorite invention, the telephone, and will call, text or message just to catch you up on things. If you get multiple messages each day from someone, they are likely a Peach. As a matter of fact, they are likely to contact you, day or night, just to tell you the latest news or to check up on you. And if they find you at home when they call they are likely to eagerly catch you up for hours, if you allow them to, telling every detail of things you might not even want to know. I sometimes tease that Peaches are why Plums and Apples sometimes don't answer their phones, but in reality the ripe Peach is a most pleasant spirit with whom to interact. A family just is not complete without at least one of these special spirits to keep everyone in touch. Indeed, the Peach is often the social glue between friends and family.

• *Loyal, compassionate, warmhearted, and loves to give advice*

The Peach is a very compassionate, friendly, and warm-hearted spirit that will always be there for others when asked. The Peach is generous with both its time and with its possessions and is very loyal to others who value their words. The Peach will go out of its way to help make others feel more comfortable. It can get very involved in other people's lives, but always with the purist of motives. The Peach is very sympathetic to others in pain and sincerely desires to help lessen this pain and often volunteers its time in the service of others. This spirit type will always jump in and try to fix situations with its vast knowledge and try to talk others through their problems.

• *Knows a little about a lot of different topics*

To some spirit types, it may appear that the Peach is somewhat superficial and is giving too much attention to small things, but this is an unfair criticism. The good natured Peach spirit is simply interested in many diverse things at a lesser level of detail than many of the other spirits which are more likely to probe deeply into a few things. In other words, while the intensity and depth of exploring specific things in its world is not as developed as that of other spirits, the Peach compensates by extensively developing the range of things with which it has knowledge. The Peach is likely to have strong feelings about many issues; it may not however, have many well-developed reasons for these opinions. Thus, as mentioned at the beginning of this chapter, the Peach spirit usually knows a little bit about a lot of different things. This trait appropriately equips the Peach for its benign encounters with other people and allows it to be successful in holding adequate conversations about almost anything with almost anyone. This enables the Peach's primary needs to be met with regularity and with great duration.

Peach Spirit Language: Words

The language of the Peach spirit is words. The Peach's world is consumed by words. It listens to the news, reads all kinds of books and magazines, and is even likely to enjoy word games in its leisure time. Of course the social media is a perfect forum for the Peach spirit to share and gain information. This spirit loves to tell you what it has learned each and every time it encounters you. Peaches communicate best with the world through verbal sharing whether one-on-one or in front of a group. Peach spirits are energized and find satisfaction in social environments that they have the opportunity and means to express, and communicate their ideas freely and without time limits. Thus, the spirit energy needed for Peaches to ripen—to become the full expression of their unique human potential—comes from roots planted in the fertile soil of a captive audience that appreciates and embraces their gift of verbal sharing.

Primary Peach Need: To be Heard

If you are a Peach, then your primary need is to be heard by others. You need people to care about you by listening to your dreams, hearing about your struggles, and paying attention to your successes. Peaches not only need to talk, but also love to talk, and can do so for hours on end without ever seeming to come up for air. The Peach needs to be heard and they accomplish this by being extremely talented speakers. They are so gifted that they can even carry the entire conversation, if necessary, as long as they think that you are listening. Thus, while the Plum believes in and responds to love and affection, the Apple to concrete rewards, the Pineapple to praise and appreciation, it should come as no surprise that the Peach believes in and responds to words. The more words the better for the Peach. In fact, the Peach cherishes words so much that when it is not talking with someone on the phone or in person, its favorite pastimes include: watching television (lots of words being said), reading (lots of words in print), writing someone a lengthy letter or e-mail, or chatting on the Internet.

Peaches also desire to be needed. Specifically, the Peach needs significant others to seek its advice and to rely upon it for input in making decisions. While the Peach is aware of proper social etiquette and does not ever wish to be improper or disrespectful, it often will offer suggestions when its advice is not solicited because of its need to be helpful and its need to be heard. It does not intend to offend, but it does want to offer the important information so that a better decision may be made. This rationale makes its unsolicited offering of advice socially appropriate, which is very important to the Peach spirit. The Peach needs a lot of attention and wants to be a valued confidante and at the same time desires to be viewed as being socially skilled by others. When it accomplishes these objectives, then it is even more likely to be sought out for advice and be heard by a maximum number of people.

Decoding Peach Relationships
Family, Friends, and Acquaintances

• *Seeks to maximize number of relationships to increase its potential audience*

It is easy to see that relationships are quite important to the Peach since relationships are the vehicle by which the Peach can be heard. Generally, rather than focusing its efforts on having a few deeply developed relationships, the Peach attempts to have many relationships. With the emphasis being on quantity, relationships for the Peach tend to be more acquaintance-type and less developed than relationships are for other spirits. Because of their innate verbal orientation and skill, the Peach is always equipped and ready to have a conversation with anyone who will listen. This may be a stranger met in a grocery store or a solicitor that visits the Peach's home (who is usually also a Peach). Bus rides, airline travel, and social transportation of any type are likely to reveal Peaches that strike up conversation with strangers as if they have known them for a lifetime. And of course the "social media" is the Peaches technology playground. A Peach is probably the creator of "chat rooms" and "blogs" on the Internet, a perfect online place for Peaches to share. Thus, while relationships for the Plum are spontaneous and deep; for the Apple they are slow and steady; and for the Pineapple they are changeable on a daily basis; for the Peach relationships are spontaneously verbal in nature and are more social in nature.

• *Has good intentions*

Remembering that the Plum is controlled by feelings, the Apple by thoughts, the Pineapple by both thoughts and feelings, the Peach is controlled by intentions, which are usually good. Birthday cards may arrive late and there may be unexpected delays in plans, but there will always be that letter or telephone call explaining every detail of the delay. Thus, the Peach spirit, in a nice way, may come across to significant others as being a bit scattered, but its personal charm, more than compensates for this appearance. Peaches are social spirits through and through, and thus are very susceptible to social pressures to conform. The latest fashion, the most recent popular diet, or the latest bestselling books are things, which the Peach must keep up with, in order to have new things to talk about with its others. You can always find a Peach in a hair salon chatting while having its hair styled, at a bar chewing the fat, at parties socializing about the latest world news, or in department stores shopping where they might run into someone with whom to talk.

• *Desires harmony in relationships*

The Peach's relationships tend to be more one dimensional, based solely on words (not deeds) that do not encourage relationships to develop to an intimate level. This is not to say that there is no depth of feelings, for Peaches are extremely loyal and loving, but they show this first and foremost in their words. The Peach spirit will write letters and lengthy e-mails expressing feelings and will always show their love by calling to check to see that you made it home safely. The Peach values harmony in relationships and will repeatedly tell you how much it loves you. It is just fine with Peaches that they do not have deep relationships demanding a lot of action-oriented behavior because truly the Peach just wants someone to talk to, and even more someone to listen.

Romantic Love Relationships

- *Romance is conducted verbally*

In romantic relationships, the Peach spirit wants a mate that will listen and with whom it can collect memories, later to be shared. The Peach will enjoy traveling, eating out, and creating social gatherings with its mate. The Peach is the ultimate social host among spirit types. But be careful of going to a movie or even church, as the Peach is likely to talk to you in those settings too. From the Peach's perspective words are more valued than deeds. In an intimate relationship the Peach has the best of intentions, but somehow may fall short of accomplishing what it had promised to do because someone else was available to listen.

- *Love to give advice*

If you are in an intimate relationship with a Peach spirit, you will be able to tell because when you ask them what they want to do with you, they most often will say, "let's talk," and before you know it they have started talking. If you do not feel like talking or perhaps, I should say listening, the Peach spirit will think something is wrong and will go on talking to you simply to find out what is wrong. If the Peach ever gets you to talk about a problem you are having, then it will give you advice. Ask a Peach any question about any problem and it will be sure to offer you much advice. Peaches will give their mate (and others) advice on proper diet and exercise, the best cure for cancer, and tell you what to believe about capital punishment. The Peach is even likely to know your daily horoscope. Sometimes, however, because of its need to be heard, the Peach will offer advice when it has not been requested, which may make it appear to be manipulative or pushy. But really, a ripe Peach spirit never intends any harm. This is true when Peaches are being superficially critical. It is simply conversation for the Peach to say that you might look better with a different hairstyle or to inform you that a particular color is not becoming to you or that you really should match your socks. When encountering this type of criticism from a Peach, it must be remembered that the Peach is extremely loyal in intimate relationships and is only offering helpful advice. The Peach will accept and love you as long as you are willing to listen and it will be very forgiving of you, if you apologize and let it talk about its perception about the event.

When the Code Goes Wrong: Obstacles to Growth and Ripening

- *May be so eager to talk that it does not actively listen to others*

Because the Peach needs to be heard so much, it often fails to fully listen to others or to let others express their feelings or thoughts. Sometimes, I say that the fuzz gets in the way of the Peach spirit hearing clearly what others may be saying or picking up on other people's cues about the conversation. It is not that the Peach does not want to listen, but its enthusiasm for sharing often overtakes its impulse control; it may even interrupt a partner with whom it is communicating. If this behavior happens often enough, other people will eventually not attempt to express themselves in the presence of the Peach spirit and at the extreme, people may begin avoiding the Peach. This avoidance behavior is highly detrimental to the Peach being able to fulfill its needs. Without having people to talk to, the Peach will feel neglected and perhaps experience depression. When alone Peaches may easily fall prey to other self-defeating behaviors like over-eating or watching too much television. Relying on such passive activities may lead to the Peach neglecting exercise, self-care, and health. Peaches often fail to create positive alone time and self-nurturing activities. They must take time for self-reflection and need to monitor their needs for sharing, as well as the input from others that may add to the quality of their life.

- *Not attuned to the positive or negative nature of what it shares*

Another problem for the Peach spirit may arise from the nature of its conversation with others, in that it either shares too much positive information or slips into sharing too much negative information with others. In the first case, a Peach can become so focused on being heard and wanting this attention that it will share much more information than is needed. Furthermore, to get other people's attention the Peach may be overly ingratiating and thus, appear insincere. The Peach spirit may have problems picking up on verbal and non-verbal cues from others and thus, may not know when to stop talking. Again, this will interfere with the Peach's need for social interaction because others will shy away from the talkative Peach.

On the other side of the coin, the Peach may be so eager to share things with other spirits that the Peach shares negative things, not with the intention to hurt, but simply to have something to say. Peaches must be extremely careful not to gossip, be negative, or strongly opinionated because once again its support network of ripe spirits will quickly diminish. Also, because the Peach itself is sensitive, it is particularly susceptible to being hurt by negative words or even constructive criticism. When another spirit criticizes something the Peach has said, it may blame the other person inappropriately, because it has been bruised. When this occurs, the Peach spirit may become even more opinionated and strongly critical of others who do not share the same Peach view. It may strike out with anger, but is more likely to impose a guilt trip on the other until the other spirit comes around to the Peach's point of view. The best advice for the Peach is the classic statement, "If you do not have something positive to say, do not say anything at all." If the Peach is perceived by others to gossip or be negatively opinionated or even worse, not to maintain confidential information, not only will its credibility and integrity be hurt, but also its source of energy—an audience—will quickly disappear.

• *Tends to be the verbal worriers*

Finally, because of their social nature, Peaches are very vulnerable to the social forces of our time that encourage people to be afraid and to worry. As already mentioned, Peaches love television, radio, and newspapers, which encourage people to worry about everything. You never know when a bomb will be dropped, or an airplane will crash, or you will come down with malaria, but you better worry about it and Peaches do. They listen to words, believe them, and then pass them on. Peaches are the greatest of worriers and need to be careful in submitting themselves to environments, which are filled with negative messages that promote worrying. To the extreme the worry can inhibit the Peach from interacting freely with its environment and making the contacts that it so much needs. Peaches need to find positive support systems which will help counterbalance the negative messages of today's media and can accomplish this by being positive themselves and spreading sincere positive words of encouragement and hope. Thus, the Peach needs to practice active listening techniques and be positive with its words to avoid obstacles, which could block the fulfillment of its need to be heard.

Putting It All Together: The Peach Spirit

The Peach's gift of the spirit is its oratory ministerial skills. When the Peach spirit is fully actualized, it will yield its fruit to the world-of inspiring and motivational oration. Its eloquence in public speaking can move both the mind and heart of any spirit and can be a powerful tool in bringing people a new awareness of their own spiritual life. Famous religious speakers like Billy Graham, Oral Roberts, and Robert Shuler demonstrated their gifts for motivation and spiritual change through their words. Outside of the institution of religion, Peaches include media figures like Walter Cronkite, Peter Jennings, Barbara Walters, and even the beloved baseball announcer Harry Caray who inspired their various audiences with unique and popular discourse. Talk show hosts like David Letterman, Oprah Winfrey, Rosie O'Donnell, Ellen DeGeneres, and Johnny Carson represent the positive power of the Peach spirit by combining humor and information to charm their audiences. Voluminous works such as those by James Michener, Shakespeare, and Tolstoy, represent Peaches that had a lot to say. Anywhere that you find a lot of words, an outgoing personality, and an affinity for positively influencing other people with their inspirational and/or entertaining words, you will find a talkative Peach spirit.

PEACH CODE SUMMARY

Distinctive Notable Attributes	Verbally expressive to others about its opinions
	Verbose in describing its experiences
	Socially extroverted and outgoing with everyone (no one is a stranger to the peach)
	Loves to learn about almost anything and translates that learning into stories to be told
Spirit Language	Words
Core Spirit Needs	To be heard as often as possible by many people
	To be needed for advice
Relationships	Loyal to friends and family who value its words
	Wants a partner to collect experiences to talk about
	Values harmony in relationships
	Is a gracious and effective host for social gatherings
Obstacles to Growth	May be so eager to talk that it does not listen
	Not skilled at attending to receptivity cues of others
	Prone to worry
Gift of the Spirit	Inspirational oratory skills

And now you can recognize the Peach spirit, read the next chapter to decode the Coconut spirit.

CHAPTER 6

Decoding The Commanding Coconut
The Commander-in-Chief Spirit

The Commanding Coconut Spirit

Hard on the outside with a very firm shell,
Winning at all costs is what it does so well.
To control its life and be admired are its main
  needs,
It does not care about your words, really only
  your deeds.

Judging and arrogant, it may outwardly appear.
It will control and dominate which may cause fear,
But please remember that it's just not all that
  tough,
Because its inside is filled with sweet white fluff.

The Coconut Spirit Comparison Worksheet

If you are a Coconut spirit you...

Feel best when you are...	acting according to your convictions
Feel the most reward...	when you are in charge of others
Feel most at ease...	with any spirit giving you unquestioned loyalty
May be seduced by...	absolute power and prestige
Avoid...	changes that require you to modify convictions
Lead by...	giving commanding orders
Follow others who are...	are higher in the chain of command
Enjoy activities ...	in which you supervise others
Cannot understand...	people who question authority
Distance yourself from...	activities led by other spirit types
Find your best friends in...	other spirits that are loyal
Most want a mate to...	follow your lead without question
Feel the most pain...	when someone or something cracks your shell and discovers your soft inside
Make the best decisions...	when acting on innate resourcefulness
Make the worst decisions...	when sticking stubbornly with old convictions
Think that you are...	the best one to make major decisions
Need to have at all times...	people to command
Know your best relationship gift is...	confident leadership

Spirit/Fruit Link

The coconut is the perfect fruit to represent this spirit. Its tough outer shell protects a very soft and flavor filled inside. Whereas the Plum, Apple, and Peach spirits relate primarily to the world through emotions, reasoning, and words respectively, the Coconut spirit relates primarily through its firm structured system of beliefs, convictions, and associated deeds. Just as the peach was selected for its juicy texture to signify its predominantly feeling dimension, the coconut was selected because its outer structural toughness nicely illustrates its predominant thinking side like the Apple. It might even be fair to say that the Coconut spirit is an extremely "hard-headed" Apple with less precision than the Apple in its analysis of information. The brown tough hairy outer shell of the coconut represents its associated spirit's strict unbending beliefs and convictions. Those encountering the Coconut spirit may find it difficult to crack this demanding, assertive, and somewhat controlling spirit. Though less frequently encountered than other spirits, the characteristics of the Coconut spirit make its presence readily apparent and visible to other spirits. Found most often in situations demanding external conformity, where authority is given by virtue of title or position, and in situations where power and toughness go with the territory, other spirits might never be aware that inside that hard outer shell is a soft vulnerable and unique individual. This combination of a tough exterior and soft interior perfectly suits the "Commanding Coconut" for it can lead others who follow to places they would never attain on their own, while protecting them with its private inner care and concern. Certainly, the Coconut spirit adds a wonderful and much needed texture and flavor to the world by its presence.

Coconut DNA (Distinct Notable Attributes)

- *Commanding leadership, authoritative orders, and demanding loyalty*

Encoded directly into the Coconut spirit's DNA is a fierce leadership gene that brings a unifying chord to previously separate working parts. Whether the head of a family, the executive director of a business organization, or Commander-in-Chief of military, this results oriented spirit will aim high on its goals for the group it leads and not be satisfied with anything but the best. And the Coconut spirit leads by example, and will not ask anything of its constituents that it has not already done.

• *Acts on convictions*

Not being motivated to think in an entirely logical way or too often feel its feelings deeply, the Coconut spirit orients itself to the world through a structured belief system and set of convictions which gives order to its world and reinforces it self-perceived position of power and authority enabling it to successfully lead others.

The Coconut is uncomfortable with human fears, weaknesses, and personal vulnerabilities. By creating a belief and value system that directly defines the Coconut's self-concept and by remaining rigidly loyal to this, the Coconut effectively walls off outward aspects of the world that represent uncertainty in order and at the same time walls in the soft feeling aspects of itself. In this way, it is able to create its own well-ordered and predictable environment and focus its energy on reaching its goals for those that it leads.

• *Wants an ordered and predictable environment*

Order and stability are key concepts that the Coconut seeks to maintain as it interacts actively with the world around it. There is little room for its inward feelings to be involved in the tough every-day decisions it must make. Too much objectivity and data from the outside world will only confuse the issue. The Coconut spirit knows best what to do based on its own experience and has built a very sophisticated, but not precisely logical set of convictions and beliefs that drive its decisions and empowers it to lead.

Coconuts dislike overweighing, analyzing, and reflecting on life as a means for deciding how, when, or why to act; thus, they willingly adopt the laws, rules, or standards of some external source. Like the Apple, they see decisions involving people more from an impersonal point of view than a personal one. Drawn to organizational structures where they are a part of something much bigger than themselves, they create a tough outer shell made up of the beliefs, practices, and principles of their chosen group, institution, or tradition. They will be loyal and rigidly adhere to these organizations as long as the power and/or prestige from this association reinforce them and their control.

Coconuts' strong personal identification with something external to themselves makes them inclined to be rather inflexible in their thinking. Coconut spirits may tend to over-generalize and stereotype because they have a strong preference for absolutes; in other words these spirits may be intolerant of and unwilling to consider ambiguity and "shades-of-gray." The power-conferring confidence that they feel from their belief system disposes Coconut spirits to be decisive and to act as if they are always right. Unlike Apples that change their decision when the facts and objective details of the situation clearly indicate that change is needed, the Coconut is not likely to change its course even when data suggest it should. It will stubbornly stick to its original decision based on its convictions.

Coconuts know what is expected of them and what they expect from others. They are not the least concerned to know or to explore the philosophical premise on which their beliefs or affiliations are based. Rarely can another spirit engage a Coconut in an argument or discussion of much depth and actually change the Coconut's opinion. Again, unlike the Apple spirit whose desire to be right results in meticulous analysis of the validity of its thoughts and the accuracy of its reasoning, the Coconut's desire to be right results in its steadfast adherence to some system of beliefs and practices deeply entrenched in its mind from experience. In reality, the Coconut actually may have given very little thought to its position. Other spirits soon learn that Coconuts may respond with a condescending reply, judgmental retort, hostile comeback, or superior remark to any spirit that questions its beliefs or decisions. Rather than mix words, the

Coconut will abruptly end the exchange and will discount the inter-action. Coconuts have pure intentions and just want things to work efficiently and this approach from their point of view is the most efficient. They give the orders and others without question should obey those orders so good results will follow.

• *Extremely confident and decisive*

The Coconut spirit is very uncomfortable with human weak-nesses, personal fears, and insecurities. These are contained deep within its shell and from the Coconut's point of view, others should do the same with their insecurities. When faced with any conflict or when in contests with others, other spirits need be aware that the Coconut expects to win. Coconut spirits are readily willing to risk insult and personal injury in a confrontation in order to defend that for which they stand; for to threaten this is to threaten their spirit, the source of their invulnerability and strength. Regardless of the out-come of battle and hard knocks given, the Coconut is hard to bruise deeply and it will find great strength and resiliency in the knowledge that comes in having remained steadfast to its principles. This atti-tude of unerring confidence is not always a source of contention. It can act as a powerful stimulus and directing influence in bringing together an unstructured or undisciplined group of people and turn-ing it into a purposeful, focused, and efficient operating unit. In this capacity, Coconuts make excellent spokespersons for special interest groups, strong-minded political activists, religious trailblazers, great military leaders, and staunch participants in the practices and activi-ties that preserve the values of middle class conventionalism.

Coconut Spirit Language: Commands

Coconut spirits demand complete loyalty by whatever group they are leading. Their language is one of commands and unques-tioned authority in which they give orders, expect quick responses, and demand positive results. While their language may seem somewhat impersonal and harsh to the more feeling spirits, they lead by doing and do not demand anything of others that they also do not demand of themselves. And like the captain of a ship, they will defend their followers with their lives. This no nonsense leadership language can quickly turn an inefficient, loosely linked group of diverse spirits into a well-oiled, efficient, and productive machine.

Primary Coconut Need: Unquestioned Authority and Loyalty

The Coconut's number one need is for authoritative control over those that it leads. It also requires unwavering loyalty form those it serves. It does not seek to be loved like the Plum. Neither is it concerned about the accuracy of its logic like the Apple or with gaining the approval of others like the Pineapple. It does not need an audience to talk to like the Peach. The desire to have power, authority, and control over loyal followers is its primary need. The Coconut spirit wants to be the captain of its own ship and will usually reward its crew with a safe passage through the rough seas of life as long its orders are followed without question. The Coconut spirit does not focus on the process of reaching a goal, but is much more of an "end justifies the means" type of leader. While it certainly takes an authoritarian and autocratic approach in this leadership, it is a hardworking and responsible spirit that will also assume total responsibility for success or even failure in reaching its group's objectives. Overall, while it is a tough leader and needs obedience from others around it, if its needs are fulfilled, this tough nut will be firm, fair, and generous to those supporting it.

Decoding Coconut Relationships
Family, Friends, and Acquaintances

• *Carries high expectations of self and others*

The particular need of each spirit type influences the nature of its relationship to the significant others in its life. In taking absolute control of its ship, the Coconut has high expectations for itself and those that it serves. At the same time, the Coconut spirit demands unwavering obedience from others it is serving.

- *Likely to impose its structure, order, and will on its significant relationships*

As in the other areas of their lives, Coconuts desire control in relationships; thus, it is their tendency to seek a power position with others. They will expect to have a significant influence on the beliefs, values, and particularly the behaviors of their associates. Coconuts expect to have others do as they say, think as they think, and value the things that the Coconut values. This spirit's need to control and direct is well-balanced in relationships with those spirits who either desire to be directed by others or who have no strong personal self-definition (i.e., beliefs, convictions, preferences) and can tolerate the Coconut's strong influence on their lives. The more timid spirits may stand in awe by the strong willed Coconut and feel reassurance in such a relationship. These less decisive spirits may be ready to jump into action, but are not sure what action to take or in which direction to jump. The Coconut is just the one to say, "jump" and will be glad to furnish the particulars of how high, when, and where. Thus, the dominance and authority the Coconut desires can be given and received in a mutually gratifying manner to complementary spirits. However, the more self-directed spirits may find themselves at odds with the Coconut spirit and experience it as being unbending, headstrong, aggressive, and overbearing.

Coconuts are not into personal sharing in relationships. In particular, they tend to be uneasy talking about the normal processes of their physical bodies and may behave as if they do not even have one. These spirits are the ones that suffer long miles on a business trip to avoid admitting the need for a rest stop and will do anything to prevent going to the doctor or even talking about physical problems. They naturally have a high threshold for pain. They also are the spirits who have contributed the most creative and fantastical answers to the question, "Where do babies come from?"

Since much of the Coconut's identity derives from the shell of its belief system, its standards become the standards of what it has chosen to represent. Usually these standards are imposed on those spirits with whom they associate. Coconut spirits are fairly set and conforming in appearance and behavior to whatever standard is the norm of their belief system. The more inwardly directed and creative spirits will rarely be compatible with the Coconut who will be totally indifferent to their love for the novel, unique, and artistic, and who will be unmoved by their quest for those experiences in life which touch the inner soul of the individual.

Romantic Love Relationships

- *Actively protects the privacy of their soft inner side from others*

In intimate relationships, the more feeling spirits be warned that Coconuts are loathed to share personal intimate things about themselves. Of all the spirits, the Coconut is the most uncomfortable with emotional and physical intimacy and often avoids these by adopting highly moralistic attitudes or by making sarcastic or scathing remarks to abruptly halt anything that gets too personal. The Coconut spirit is most likely to divert intimate conversations or actions away from the feeling domain by making fun of feelings brought up by the activity or suggesting that others are being "too sensitive." The Coconut is likely to do this when, in fact, the conversation or activity is in reality hitting "too close" to the Coconut's soft inner core. More than anything it does not want its protective shell to be cracked and share this softness in front of others.

The Coconut has little need to share any more than its tough outer shell with others. Some spirits are able to exist in a prolonged relationship with a Coconut and to eventually work their way under its shell. These spirits will be the rare individuals who will discover the soft nature inside the Coconut; the vulnerable and sensitive individual that has used its hard shell often to protect itself against the harsh realities of an often impersonal world.

• *Is loyal, dependable, and hardworking*

Those intimate with a Coconut spirit will experience a loyal and dependable spirit that works long and hard for that which it believes in, including friends and spouses who have shown their good faith and loyalty to the Coconut. And the Coconut will selflessly share whatever rewards it achieves from its successes with those who have faithfully supported its ways and efforts. For those spirits that do experience the inside of the Coconut, I recommend that it might be wise not to let the Coconut know that you have seen its soft inside beneath the shell. If the Coconut feels that its shell is not secure, it will be motivated to reinforce it and thus, the avenue of personal intimacy might be closed.

When the Code Goes Wrong: Obstacles to Growth and Ripening

• *Natural resistance to change*

Like each of the other spirits, the Coconut has weaknesses or blind spots particular to its unique spirit. Most of the Coconut's blind spots revolve around its desire to be in control and to have others obey its commands without question. One blind spot likely to show up in terms of impatience, anger, or even outrage on the part of the Coconut is when the order of its environment is changed in any way. Coconuts do not like change. In fact, they seem to have a natural resistance to it. A well-intentioned person who cleans up the Coconut's cluttered desk is likely to receive an explosive outburst from the Coconut instead of a thank you. When Coconut spirits take their control to an extreme, they can become totally inflexible, close-minded, and not think about the good intentions that others may have in contributing to the change. If the change is not initiated by the Coconut, it will likely attempt to return things back to the status quo even if that is not in the best interest of itself and others. Along with this blind spot is a related problem; Coconuts do not like surprises. They want their environment to be predictable and ordered from their point of view; Coconuts are not well prepared to deal with surprises of any kind. They may even view the surprise changes as disasters.

- *May run over people in an effort to reach its goals*

Another obstacle for the Coconut spirit is that in its effort to be the captain of its ship both at home and at work, it may unintentionally run people over that it cares about in its effort to reach goals and fulfill needs. It may get so goal oriented that it becomes a workaholic and not notice the impact it is having on its family. Or it may be so rigid and demanding of others that it never considers their feelings or point of view in making decisions. Coconuts may unintentionally invalidate and disempower those who have been faithfully serving them. Coconuts must remember that a good captain knows its crew and validates their effort often and sincerely to make the crew even more effective. Leadership by task performance without an interpersonal component will usually result in a poorly sustained effort by those individuals being led.

- *May be blind to its internal soft inside*

Finally, a word must be said about the Coconut's blind spot to its own inside softness. Coconuts work so hard to build the thick outer shell that protects their soft vulnerable inside that even they are not fully aware of the strength of feelings and emotions that lie within that shell. Coconut spirits assume that people will only see their outside and never discover their inside. However, most Coconut spirits do usually crack for someone at some time in their life. It may be a loving family member or pet that cracks that tough exterior with unconditional love; or it may be an external crisis such as the unexpected loss of a loved one or job, or a serious health condition like a heart attack or cancer that cracks its shell and exposes the soft fluffy inside of the Coconut. If unprepared for this exposure, the Coconut can go through a very traumatic identity crisis as others reach out in different ways to provide support. The commanding Coconut that has previously been totally in charge of the giving process may not be prepared to receive from others and be treated gently. Ideally, the ripe Coconut will create a safety net of one or two trusted spirits to share itself with fully as it captains its ship in life.

Putting It All Together: The Coconut Spirit

The Coconut spirit is a complex and intriguing spirit. It loves being in command and creating a working team that can attain high goals. It expects loyalty from all it serves and will unselfishly give all of its energy to champion the group's cause. Overall, if the Coconut can self-monitor its demanding behavior of others to ensure that both the intention of the demand and the value of the person being commanded are clear, it can be an incredibly effective and highly successful leader. At the same time, the Coconut spirit must be aware of and allow one or two spirits to recognize and meet the needs of its soft inside. With this in place the Coconut can guide others successfully and negotiate some of life's most challenging roads. Military leaders like Ulysses S. Grant, Douglas MacArthur, George Patton; political leaders like Winston Churchill, Franklin Roosevelt, Margaret Thatcher; and inspirational change leaders like Marie Curie, Rosa Parks, Gloria Steinem, and Florence Nightingale are among the many special people whose commanding leadership actions left a permanent positive Coconut spirit imprint upon history. And the Coconut spirit is often used to entertain us with characters like Archie Bunker, Captain Ahab, Captain Kirk, and perhaps most famous of all, Scrooge. The Coconut's ultimate gift is its faithfulness to the convictions, principles, and team that it represents. It is a deserving "Captain of the ship" of the spirit types.

COCONUT CODE SUMMARY

Distinct Notable Attributes	Provides powerful leadership, gives authoritative orders, and demands loyalty from those it serves
	Confident, decisive, and acts on convictions
	Requires an ordered and predictable environment
Spirit Language	Commands
Core Spirit Needs	Unquestioned authority and loyalty
Relationships	Carries high expectations of self and others
	May impose its beliefs, expectations, and will on others
	Is direct, honest, and blunt in conveying feedback
Obstacles to Growth	Natural resistance to change
	May run over people to reach its goals
	May be blind to its internal soft inside
Gift of the Spirit	Faithfulness to its convictions and the people it serves

And now the Coconut spirit has been revealed, read the next chapter to decode the Banana spirit…

CHAPTER 7

Decoding the Belonging Banana
The Serving Spirit

The Belonging Banana Spirit

The Banana is a nice quiet fruit,
It's shy and passive and awfully cute.
Affectionate and kind, it likes to be,
Needing to fit in is its prime key.

It likes hanging around in a great big bunch,
It may even follow you out to lunch;
Adapting to each person is its scheme,
Its life is lived with a social service theme.

The Banana Spirit Comparison Worksheet

If you are a Banana spirit you…

Feel best when you are…	surrounded by other Bananas
Feel the most reward…	being part of a productive team
Feel most at ease…	in highly predictable environments
May be seduced by…	assertive spirits asking for your help
Avoid…	leadership positions and activities
Lead by…	steadfast and consistent work
Follow others who are…	appreciative of your service
Enjoy activities that are…	ordered, routine, and structured
Cannot understand…	wanting to stand out in a crowd
Distance yourself from…	leadership positions
Find your best friends in…	other Bananas
Most want a mate to…	let you fit into its life
Feel the most pain…	when being singled out (for praise or criticism)
Make the best decisions…	based on what is best for the group
Make the worst decisions…	when alone
Think that you are…	adaptable and positive
Need to have at all times…	others around for support
Know your best relationship gift is…	an adaptability to follow others' lead

Spirit/Fruit Link

Following in line after the rest of the spirits, but not wanting to be the last one described is the Banana spirit. Perhaps, I should say Bananas because like the fruit for which it is named, these spirits are usually found hanging around in bunches. The banana represents this spirit precisely for several reasons. First, when bananas are ripe, they have a cheerful bright yellow color that is pleasant to the eye. Also, bananas need to be used or their skin will quickly turn black and the fruit inside will rot. And so it is that Banana spirits have a core desire to be part of a group, to be needed by that group, and to have an immediate connection with others in performing the tasks of the group. Finally, bananas as a fruit can be prepared to eat in many different ways. They can be eaten whole or they can be split, sliced, or even mashed; they always retain that distinctive texture and taste that is appealing to so many people. Likewise, the Banana spirit is very adaptable to different spirits and situations, fills many different gaps in our culture and others, and successfully provides its same distinctive flavor to those around it regardless of how or who it serves.

Banana DNA (Distinct Notable Attributes)

• *Hangs around in bunches for support*

Bananas are the group spirit. While they can function effectively in an independent mode, their preference and their motivation is to be part of a team with a lot of other Bananas for support. Whether it is at work, home, or at play the Banana will always try to find other Bananas just to hang with. This serves two basic purposes. First, they find a special kind of support from the other like spirits that they hang around with that helps fulfill their strong need for belonging and validation. Secondly, Bananas also hang around with other Banana spirits because they actually function more efficiently in this group rather than alone. Only another Banana spirit can truly understand a Banana's needs and provide just the right kind of support. The Banana spirit has no need to be the center of attention as an individual, but prefers to bask in the warmth of a team victory or a successful group project. A team of Bananas under the right leadership can be incredibly effective for the right task. For Bananas, the whole bunch is really more than the sum of their individual spirits.

- *Prefers order and routine*

Banana spirits might be best thought of as the "followers" of our spirit types. Bananas are excellent followers and do not mind taking orders from the Apple or Coconut leader. They can be bruised if they do not perceive themselves as fitting into their present environment successfully and making at least some significant contribution to the group outcome. This gentle spirit is practical and likes order and routine. The more it can follow a predictable routine to provide its contribution to the group, the better for the Banana spirit. It thrives on schedules and likes to know what is expected of it each day. Rather than writing a feeling diary like the Plum, the Banana usually has a routine time budget plan which it follows each day to keep it organized.

- *Does not have strong opinions or convictions*

The Banana spirit does not usually hold strong opinions on anything and may even appear somewhat wishy-washy in terms of its beliefs. This is simply because the Banana does not really care about being right like the Apple; it only wants to fit into the social order around it. Sometimes the Banana may appear to act without thinking (which is particularly offensive to the Apples of the world), but in truth, the Banana is acting on its keen perceptions of the world and not on its thoughts about those perceptions. The Banana is quite content to allow the Apples and Coconuts of the world to argue about what the correct answers to the world's problems are, and as soon as they figure it out, the Banana will be the first spirit to follow their advice. Thus, it might be fair to say that Bananas avoid conflicts and controversy caused by thinking which also makes it rare for them to offer new ideas or opinions.

Banana Spirit Language: Service

The Banana spirit is energized by its desire to humbly serve others. Thus, while the Plum resonates to feelings, the Apple to thoughts, the Pineapple to both thoughts and feelings, the Peach to words, the Coconut to convictions, the gentle Banana language is one of service. The Banana's finely tuned perceptions serve it well in being an extremely versatile chameleon in moving between its feeling and thinking dimensions allowing it to perceive what kind of service is needed. In the name of service, it maintains effective and productive relationships with other team members. And it is these supportive relationships that in turn supply the power and motivation for the Banana to add its significant service contribution to the group.

Primary Banana Need: To Fit in and Belong

The primary need of the Banana spirit is to fit into and belong to a group or team. It meets this need by following the lead of those around it and by often imitating them and adopting the values and interests of others so that it will appear to fit. The Banana's need is not for control, love, approval, verbal attention, or correctness; it just wants strongly to belong and to contribute to its group(s). Thus, like the pliable and malleable fruit for which it is named, the Banana will bend, split, slice and squeeze itself to fit into the environment in which it currently places itself. Because of its powerful need to fit in, the Banana spirit has developed an acute ability to assess, understand, and even anticipate the needs of others in its environment. When it is moved to a new environment, it quickly and precisely determines how it can best adapt to once again seamlessly fit-in. Then like a chameleon, it changes, conforms, and contributes very positively to the new environment by filling significant gaps in the new system giving it a place and reason to belong. It still keeps its core identifying texture, but in the new system it may appear to be very different to previous spirit associates because of its apparently new beliefs and opinions that always match those of the current group. Also, when moving to a new environment, the Banana spirit will quickly seek out other Banana spirits for support. It does not want to be alone for long in a new setting. For it, the best spirits to hang around with first are other versatile Bananas.

Decoding Banana Relationships
Family, Friends, and Acquaintances

- *Enjoys the passive, non-leadership role in its relationships with others*

The Banana spirit by its nature is passive and mostly submissive in its relationships with others; it usually follows along with anything that others want. It does not follow to gain approval like the Pineapple, but rather it enjoys the background role, and in particular in not having the responsibility for leadership or having the spotlight shine on it in relationships. It likes to hang out with family and friends and will actively participate in any and all group functions. Bananas do most of the preparations for family reunions and will be faithful communicators with close friends.

- *Responds best to positive group appreciation*

At work the Banana's social need is merely to have its presence appreciated by others as a member of the entire group. It follows orders well and is completely trustworthy. Bananas make excellent employees anywhere that they can be given a list of tasks to do, other friendly Bananas to work with, and know exactly what is expected of them.

Romantic Love Relationships

- *May take a little time to open up to other fruit as it assesses their needs*

The Banana spirit can adapt to or have a successful relationship with any kind of spirit, but does best when it knows exactly what is expected of it. While the Banana spirit may appear timid in the early stages of a potential intimate relationship, in reality, it is actively investigating its perceptions of the partner's needs for the relationship. Once it has assessed those needs, it will be much more outgoing, cheerful, and friendly. In other words, the Banana may take a little time to open up to others, but once it does, it is quick to add its special flavor to the relationship.

- *One of the most other-centered relationship partners*

The Banana is one of the most other-centered spirits, and it will return love usually in the way it is given. If a Plum gives a Banana a hug, it will return the hug. If a Pineapple gives it praise, it will praise the Pineapple. Presents will be exchanged with the Apple and words exchanged with the Peach. And of course the Banana will faithfully serve the Coconut. The Banana will be content and extremely loyal as long it perceives that is has fit in and is both needed and useful to the spirit in relationship to it.

Overall, in relationships, the Banana is an easy spirit to please, since all it desires is to successfully fit into others' lives in meaningful ways.

When the Code Goes Wrong: Obstacles to Growth and Ripening

- *May make promises it cannot keep just because it wants to fit in so much*

The Banana's difficulties primarily stem from its need to fit in to the lifestyle and social environment of others. It desires to fit in so much that sometimes it will agree with any commitment, promise or deadline, even if it is impossible to accomplish. Thus, it is not uncommon for the Banana to be overcommitted with its time in its attempts to fit in by satisfying the wishes of others. At these times of over-commitment, it usually neglects is own self-care and may still not finish its tasks. Other spirits may not appreciate the Banana's supreme effort, because they only judge the final product. When the lack of accomplishment is added to what appears to be the Banana's wishy-washy persona, the Banana may be rejected. Rejection causes the sensitive Banana to socially bruise and be severely hurt.

- *May be overly dependent on one primary group support system*

A second problem may appear because Bananas work so hard to fit into one setting that they usually do not have other support settings available to them when they are rejected by the one into which they put their focused time and effort. Thus, when rejected by one setting, they may not have another one available for support. The Banana spirit does not fend well alone. Thus, it is imperative that each Banana utilizes its special talents to fit in with and contribute to as many environments as possible so that their network of resources is maximized.

- *Often lacks assertiveness skills; may be used by other more assertive spirits*

A prime obstacle for Banana spirits is their lack of assertiveness. They can easily be run over or used by other hard pressing spirits. Bananas may be over-worked and not complain, because they do not want to cause any waves and so much want to belong. Others may know that Bananas are passive and may consciously or even unknowingly take advantage of the Banana's tender and hardworking nature. At the extreme, the Banana spirit could even become the innocent scapegoat for work not accomplished by overripe spirits. The Banana spirit should periodically reevaluate those spirits that it is in relationship with to assure that it is not being misused and that indeed it is fitting into and contributing its gifts to a healthy environment.

- *Needs to be cautious of promotions*

Bananas also need to be extremely cautious of the old "Peter Principle"—the idea that individuals are elevated to their level of incompetence. Because Banana spirits are efficient at routine tasks and take orders well, they may be selected for promotions to higher levels with still more expectations. Bananas would do well to simply stick with the tasks they enjoy, stay with the group that feels comfortable, and be content.

Putting It All Together: The Banana Spirit

The Banana is the most adaptable spirit of all. Because its primary need is to fit in wherever it might find itself, the Banana is the perfect spirit for the ever-increasing diversity of American society. The Banana's gift of the spirit is its willingness to serve and be a faithful follower without a desire or need for power or recognition. Leaders can only lead if they have faithful followers and the Banana spirit is the best spirit in this arena. Once the humble Banana identifies its spiritual path of service, it can have a powerful impact on the world. It was the nameless Banana soldiers in the Revolutionary War, the Civil War, World War I, and World War II that changed the course of history and won the cause for freedom. It is Bananas that form the backbone of the workforce, the engine driving business and industry across the world. They are the steel, brick, and mortar that make the skyline possible; they are the workers that raise the skyscraper. Bananas in countless numbers keep the many institutions that service the populations up and running. Wherever there is charitable work to be done, Bananas will be the first to volunteer, providing ample support for any multitude of causes that forward social progress and benefit humanity. Bananas will be staffing the rescue and first aid stations, search-and-rescue missions, and handing out food at food banks during a crisis, or you will find them across the globe working for enterprises that service people, animals, or environments. Thus, this gentle, orderly spirit can be found throughout our society, performing great quantities of spirit-filled work and wanting as its only reward to just serve and belong. And certainly our society is a "bunch" better because of the wonderful Banana spirit and its gifts of service. If the Bible statement is right, "so the last shall be the first, and the first last..." (Mathew 20:16 KJV) then these humble service-minded Bananas will be at the head of the line at the pearly gates to Heaven.

BANANA CODE SUMMARY

Distinct Notable Attributes	Hangs around in bunches with other Bananas
	Quietly likes to be part of a team effort
	Likes to be in the "following" role
	Versatility and adaptability
	Skilled in assessing interpersonal cues
Spirit Language	Service
Core Spirit Needs	To belong and contribute its talents to groups
	To have freedom to change as its environment changes
	To be given clear directions for tasks
Relationships	Enjoys the non-leadership role in relationships
	Responds best to positive attention from others
	Passive in relationships until it identifies their partner's needs
Obstacles to Growth	May make promises it cannot keep
	Lacks assertiveness; may be run over by more aggressive spirits
	May become overly dependent on one group
Gift of the Spirit	Humility and social service

And now you have decoded the Banana spirit, read the next chapter to decode the Orange.

CHAPTER 8

Decoding The Fearless Orange
The Adventurous Spirit

The Fearless Orange Spirit

The Orange is outgoing in every way,
It prefers an adventure every day,
Experiencing all things so much anew,
Without a challenge it knows not what to do,

Active and always looking for change,
Sailing on wind or climbing a mountain range,
Life to the Orange is an adventure to live,
High adrenaline energy is what it has to give.

The Orange Spirit Comparison Worksheet

If you are an Orange spirit you...

Feel best when you are...	challenging your personal limits
Feel the most reward...	when you master a new physical challenge
Feel most at ease...	exploring new environments
May be seduced by...	challenges or dares from others
Avoid...	routine indoor sedentary activities
Lead by...	doing, rather than thinking, talking, or feeling
Follow others who...	physically and psychologically challenge you
Enjoy activities that...	produce adrenaline rushes
Cannot understand...	letting work interfere with thrilling activities
Distance yourself from...	sedentary people and activities
Find your best friends in...	other spirits that want to go for the gusto
Most want a mate to...	support your need for excitement
Feel the most pain...	when not being able to be physically active
Make the best decisions...	when acting in the moment
Make the worst decisions...	when forced to analyze all the costs and benefits
Think that you are...	here to try as many experiences as possible
Need to have at all times...	freedom to explore the natural world
Know your best relationship gift is...	a passion for active experiences

Spirit/Fruit Link

A number of popular quotes such as "Go for the gusto!" and "Eat, drink and be merry…" and of course "Carpe Diem" may have been coined for the Orange spirit. The orange was chosen as the fruit to represent this spirit because it has a vivid, bright color, a zesty flavor, and is packed with juice in multiple compartments to provide quick energy. Being the most energetic of the spirit types, the Orange spirit is in a constant search for new sources of sensory experience. Oranges are always experience oriented; the most distinguishing trait of this spirit is that it sees life as a playground for widely varying challenges and discovery. The multiple sections of the fruit provide a perfect analogy for the many separate experiences Oranges pursue. The Orange spirit lives in a perpetual quest to touch, taste, see, smell, hear, and push its senses and its body to their limits. It is no surprise to note that there is a high population density of Orange spirits living in the sunny playground states of our country, especially Florida and California, where coincidentally the linked fruit also grows best. But of course anywhere Oranges can perform challenging activities to push themselves to their physical and emotional limits is where you will find Orange spirits. Adventure and excitement, to the extreme, feed the Orange spirit.

Orange DNA (Distinct Notable Attributes)

• *Is motivated by exciting, thrilling, and risky challenges*

Unlike the Plum that is motivated by feelings, the Apple by reasoning, the Peach by words, the Pineapple by pleasing, the Coconut by power and authority, the Banana by social belonging, the Orange is motivated by any sensory stimulation that excites, thrills, and challenges. As stated, Orange spirits are experience-oriented, a characteristic which compels them to employ courage, cunning, and personal resourcefulness in meeting and/or mastering the demands of life on the "razor's edge."

In ages past, Oranges have been the hunters, explorers, and sur-vivors who waged battle with the elements to carve out an existence and who risked giant sea-monsters to sail to new lands. Nowadays, these adventure seeking spirits climb steep mountain sides, leap from aircraft, hand-glide on large kites, race speedy cars, fly into outer space, have lunch fifty stories high on steel girders, and are entrepre-neurs who take long-shot business ventures. Oranges are the spirits' risk takers, record breakers, and first responders to life's challenges.

- *A spirit of invulnerability and invincibility*

By its nature, the experience-oriented Orange quickly becomes tough, firm, and resistant to bruising. And when they bruise, the bruise just becomes a positive memento of a worthwhile experience. The physical body is to be used and pushed to its limits according to the Orange. A spirit of invulnerability and invincibility allows Oranges to range far and wide into the physical and mental worlds in their quest for new frontiers, new experiences, or in a word, adventure.

- *Fun-loving with insatiable curiosity*

The Orange is a dynamic individual who is fun and interesting to know. Ripe Orange spirits are filled with the sunshine exuberance of life, have a happy disposition, are positive and outgoing, and usu-ally possess a good sense of humor. They get along well with most other spirits and are generally very likable.

Beginning early in childhood, Oranges mark themselves with an attitude of independence and insatiable curiosity about everything. Often the last of several children, the Orange has to learn to compete for attention and family resources. Their creativity and unwillingness to conform to the socialization patterns exemplified by older siblings can cause parents to wonder if the stork dropped the wrong baby down their chimney.

The young Orange is always on the move (or roll, as is often the case!), exploring and getting into things. It is common for them to have little fear of anything. This trait disposes them to accident proneness as their life-long quest to test limits and explore the untried leads to rough-and-tumble knocks.

- *Actively learns by doing and experiencing*

Oranges learn by doing and by experiencing. To an Orange spirit, experience (hands on, feet-on, body-on) is the only qualified teacher of what it desires to learn. The student Orange may often be restless and inattentive in the formal classroom setting where emphasis is on words and "thinking" about things. Oranges are usually bright and clever, but they do not like rote learning situations. They want an education through high risks that would cause the fainter hearted spirit to quake, but which only spurs the Orange on to higher adventure. Where anxiety and fear about the future often limits other spirits, the present-oriented Orange deals with the here-and-now and is not burdened with "what-ifs." If uncomfortable anxiety should arise, the Orange dissipates it through action. If scrapes and injuries do happen, the Orange spirit may value them as badges of courage and daring. A Plum with a broken arm will be content to say it fell and broke its arm, waiting for sympathy and solicitation. An Apple will describe rationally the cause of the accident perhaps by stating, "Anyone should know that condensation on that sort of surface could cause slipping!" The Pineapple will say, "I knew if I tried that slope, I would fall, but I just wanted to do it once so my instructor would be pleased that I had been practicing." The Peach will go right to its own personal interpretation of the event in providing great detail by saying, "I saw the car pull out as I began to back up. The man must have been totally blind not to see me. There was no time to honk my horn. It happened so fast that I did not feel anything until later. I had to get out. My car is ruined. He just sat there. People everywhere were just gawking…." And the Bananas will hang around and support each other and probably never break an arm. Contrasted with these explanations, the Orange will usually quip, "Oh, just a little souvenir from my 2000 foot jump. Put a few scratches on my kite, too." And those who scold an Orange for its reckless escapades may receive a response that makes the point, "If you haven't tried it, don't knock it!"

- *Independent and nonconforming*

The stouthearted and fearless Orange does not endure the pressure of social responsibility as well as it does that of the ocean at forty feet down. Striving to be free moving to roll in any direction, restrictions that strap the Orange spirit down are poorly tolerated. They invest fully as far as time, money, and energy in their current passion of the moment, often overlooking other commitments made previously in the fire of enthusiasm that has now cooled as another experience presented itself. For example, an Orange spirit might commit to teach a course for a university until it is offered a chance to hike across the Alps. If the time commitments conflict, you can be sure the Orange will be hiking across the Alps, while someone else teaches the class.

Messiness is as natural to an Orange as orderliness is to an Apple. Though Orange spirits may pick nice apartment complexes or neighborhoods in which to live, they may not regard the tidy upkeep of porches, driveways, carports, and garages as applicable to their place. Caught up in a life of numerous interests and social involvements, Oranges may let things slide around the home place, causing much distress to neighbors. The house or apartment may serve only as a stop-off place to sleep, shower, and change. Unwashed dishes and mixed piles of clean and soiled clothing can often be found amidst an impressive store of recreational survival equipment. An Orange's garage or carport may be filled with any wide array of trendy transportation devices it can afford—sports cars, recreational vehicles, motorcycles, boats, hand-gliders, skateboards, and surfboards. A week's worth of mail may collect on its desk waiting for the Orange to slow down long enough to sort through it.

- *Great in emergency situations*

Oranges are quick to react. Being constantly alert for sensations, their finely tuned senses can respond immediately to a variety of simultaneous sensory information. Thus, Oranges are adept in responding rapidly and taking action in an emergency or crisis situation; they are able to size up the situation in an instant and act without the interference of emotions or having to think through all the aspects and possibilities. Liking challenge, Oranges are usually at their best when it seems there is no hope or solution; with its quick analysis and creative ingenuity the Orange can often provide instant assistance.

Orange Spirit Language: Adventure

Oranges have an unquenchable thirst for adventure and adrenaline rushes that creates a love for experiential learning. They connect to others based on their active life experiences and will join any group seeking new exciting adventures. Oranges will discuss their recent quests with you, but are more likely to share future plans, especially ones that forge new frontiers. Test pilots, astronauts, race drivers, and white water raft guides are all likely to be Orange spirits.

Primary Orange Need: Diverse Adrenaline Producing Experiences

The Orange's number one need is to expose itself to and be an active player in as many diverse, multi-sensory experiences as possible. The Orange is eager to learn about and define itself in terms of the experiences in life in which it participates. Risk and challenge or any situation, which is highly stimulating, particularly adrenaline producing ones, are the primary types of experiences Orange spirits seek. Simply having participated in an experience is usually not fully satisfying to the Orange. The only meaningful reward for the Orange is mastering each experience and then moving onto a higher level of proficiency of that activity or onto a totally different challenge. The best challenges to the Orange are those that are both physically and mentally challenging. Perhaps, most important in terms of life needs for the active Orange is to have freedom to pursue these challenges and the best freedom for the Orange is to have few permanent structured time commitments that take it away from its true experiential passions. It needs to be flexible about its commitments; so you may find a very bright Orange working in a candy shop in Colorado so that it may master the expert slopes in downhill skiing.

Decoding Orange Relationships
Family, Friends, and Acquaintances

- *Enthusiastic and often socially admired by others for their daring*

The very social, charming, and bursting with goodwill Orange is much admired, well thought of, and popular in friendships among the different spirits. Family members that support the Orange's quest for experiences are welcomed to the Orange's inner circle, but those that are fearful and non-supportive are quickly cast aside. Oranges view family systems and friends as part of their quest for experiences. Shared experiences give birth to new friends. It is rare to find an Orange isolated for long. It will seek other Oranges to share new experiences.

Not liking the hustle and bustle of crowded places, the Orange may wander to remote places, returning frequently to touch base with its family or friends in congenial camaraderie at its favorite hangout.

- *Relationships are experiences to lift up, not responsibilities to tie down*

Oranges are adaptable and well versed in a wide variety of role behaviors. For example, the Orange spirit can be very traditional if it suits it to be at the moment. At a family reunion, the Orange may be gracious and congenial, sincerely attentive to all the family activities, while tossing children on its knee (and across the room); later that evening, the same Orange will be out dancing in free abandon at its favorite club. Relationships for the Orange are simply diverse experiences that should lift up, not responsibilities to tie them down,

- *Friends and acquaintances are those who share action experiences*

Also, typical of Orange spirits is that they respond to their own inward direction rather than to external pressures of time schedules, others' expectations of them, or others' feelings. Viewing feelings as the responsibility of the individual having them, the Orange may seem indifferent (and often really is) to the sharing of emotional things. However, if the Orange is upset, angry or enthusiastic, others will certainly hear about it. And when the Orange is ready to go or has an engagement, it will just expect anyone else involved to be sensitive to its time schedule. The spontaneous Orange may even make plans to do something including others without consulting them. It is the Orange that will get you involved in a white water rafting trip even though you never knew there was such a thing.

Oranges are free spending and may even be generous with others, but tend to be more often on the taking side from others as they make arrangements for their adventures. An Orange may borrow an item it suddenly needs without asking or it may make a meal from the contents of another's refrigerator, while graciously asking the provider to please join in the feast. Oranges may forgo the payment of current bills in order to put a down payment on scuba gear. Thus, to many spirits, the Orange may seem self-centered, inconsiderate, unreliable, imprudent, and undependable. Scolding, fussing, or nagging will not change an Orange spirit's ways, it will only exhaust the other spirit. An Orange will be an Orange and those with Orange friends know that for all their peculiarities, the Orange spirit is positively infectious.

- *Self-aware and congenial with most spirits*

Oranges are able to get along with most spirits. In general, Orange relationships with other spirits are congenial, but if a strain occurs, it is usually a minimal one due to basic differences between itself and each of the various spirits. Specifically, Oranges respect Apples, but are likely to view them as too stiff, structured, and "frumpy." They will lend a patient ear to the Peach for a polite period of time and then move on abruptly. They regard Plums with fascination, but tend to think that they are mushy sentimentalists who are too insecure to really live. Pineapples are okay, but Oranges may become impatient with their inability to sort out their thoughts from their feelings. Also, the Pineapples need to please others is foreign to the Orange spirit. Bananas are regarded as "all right" and "good old' spirits" because they are susceptible to influence by Oranges and because they admire Oranges greatly. The diplomatic tendencies of the Orange may put it at odds with the Coconut that takes much of its identity from something outside itself. In contrast, Oranges are self-made spirits that do not berate and downgrade others who think or feel differently than they do.

Romantic Love Relationships

• *Enjoy the opening of intimate relationships*

Unlike Plums, Oranges are not romantics with hearts searching for love. Though the Orange is not beyond the sting of Cupid's arrow should it spot a kindred spirit dangling from a rock precipice on a thin line of rope, the Orange is not well suited for the responsibility and commitments of traditional marriage and family relationships. More non-traditional companion type of partnerships fit the Orange's active lifestyle better. It is experiences first and relationships second for the thrill seeking orange. Relationships are games of fun and challenge for the Orange spirit. They usually have good intentions in relationships, but their moment-to-moment focus on life can make them seem less so. Orange spirits love the opening of relationships because openings are so full of new experiences. In fact, it is often the case that Oranges go through a series of openings with different people or even the same person rather than moving on more to the deeper stages of involvement. They will often move away from a solitary relationship for some period of time in order that they may come back to that relationship as if it were a new opening. Other spirits should become acquainted with the Orange's basic nature, or they may often be confused, disappointed, or hurt while trying to win an Orange's heart and attempting to move the Orange past the initial opening stage of the relationship. The most important thing to remember is that the Orange's heart belongs to the experiences of life, of which relationships are only a part, but not the whole.

In brief, other spirits should fully experience Orange spirits, appreciate, and have fun with them. But before hearing wedding bells ringing, get to know the Orange just as it is, for it will continue to be an Orange, marriage or not. Those spirits seeking a stable, predictable, and secure relationship might do best to keep Oranges as best friends and recreational buddies.

When the Code Goes Wrong: Obstacles to Growth and Ripening

- *Susceptible to challenges, dares, and anything new*

Most of the Orange's blind spots and obstacles occur because of its total focus on the present. It may not fully anticipate long-range consequences of its actions and may take risks, which are unnecessarily dangerous to both itself and others around it. The Orange spirit is also very susceptible to challenges and dares, and may hurt itself severely in the process of meeting the challenge. For example, the Orange may be dared to do an activity that exceeds the safety limits of the equipment needed for that activity. If the equipment fails, the Orange may suffer serious bodily and/or psychological damage that will permanently inhibit its primary need for other adventures in the future.

- *Impulsive and does not anticipate the consequences of its actions*

A second closely related issue of concern for the Orange is that it does act impulsively. While in some cases this might be an advantage, such as emergency situations, it often can be detrimental in everyday non-threatening situations. Again, the Orange spirit may get itself or others severely hurt, by acting without thinking. For example, the Orange may be so involved in the present moment of a relationship that it does not think to take the responsibility for birth control. Obviously, the consequences could be serious. Thus, it is wise for the Orange spirit to moderate its impulses for experiences by practicing just a bit of rational thinking before acting.

- *May not consider that other spirits have different needs*

Finally, a third major obstacle for the Orange is its lack of awareness that other spirits may not desire the Orange's experiences. The Orange is often so carried away seeking experiences that produce adrenaline rushes that they do not consider that others who may be sharing the experience with them are doing so for different reasons and may not want to run the same risks that the Orange desires. Oranges need to be aware when there are non-Oranges engaging in Orange type of activities to moderate the risk appropriately so that other spirits may safely enjoy the activity and gather their own meaning from that activity.

Putting It All Together: The Fearless Orange

The thrill-seeking Orange spirit teaches us to push our limits, take risks, and leads by creating adventures and challenges. This positive active spirit is enthusiastic about life and sees each day as full of new adventure possibilities from which to learn and grow.

The Orange's gift of the spirit is its passionate activism. When ripened in the sunshine of spiritual light, the adventurous Orange can be the ignition for powerful spiritual movement. From Moses leading his people to the Promised Land, to John the Baptist preparing the way in the wilderness for Christ's arrival, Oranges have been powerful catalysts for change in religion. But even outside of formal religion the Orange spirit can be readily seen in activist groups like

Greenpeace, PETA, Earth First, and Habitat for Humanity. Explorers in all types of vessels like Christopher Columbus, Jacques Cousteau, Amelia Earhart, and Neil Armstrong reflect the fearless spirit of the Orange. And even today the media still pays special homage to fictional super heroes like James Bond, Superman, Wonder Woman and so many others. Popular television shows like *Survivor*, or *MacGyver* remind us of just how powerful and willing for adventure the Orange spirit can be. Indeed, Oranges have helped humanity cross into many new exciting frontiers.

ORANGE CODE SUMMARY

Distinct Notable Attributes	Is motivated by exciting, thrilling, and risky challenges
	Has a spirit of invulnerability and invincibility
	Fun-loving with insatiable curiosity
	Actively learns by doing and experiencing
	Independent, non-conforming spirit
Spirit Language	Adventure
Core Spirit Need	Diverse adrenaline producing experiences
Relationships	Enthusiastic and often socially admired for their daring
	Social connections are experiences to lift up, not responsibilities to tie down
	Friends are those who share action experiences
	Self-aware and congenial with most spirits
Obstacles to Growth	Susceptible to challenges, dares, and anything new
	Impulsive
	May not anticipate the consequences of its actions
	May not consider that other spirits have different needs
Gift of the Spirit	Passionate Activism

Now let's go a bit deeper and decipher your unique Spirit code "blend" in chapter 9.

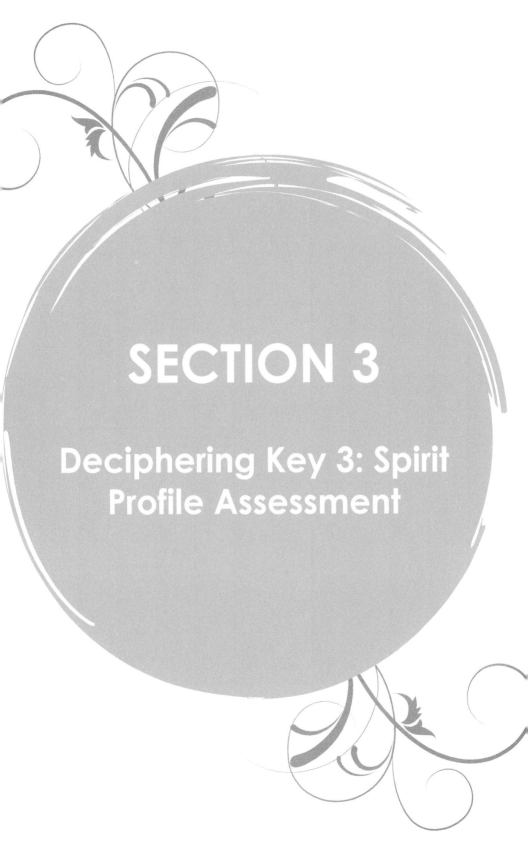

SECTION 3

Deciphering Key 3: Spirit Profile Assessment

Most of us remain strangers to ourselves, hiding who we are, and ask other strangers, hiding who they are, to love us.

—Leo Buscaglia

CHAPTER 9

Fruit Salad, Anyone?
Blended Spirits

Fruit Salad, Anyone?

Now that you have just finished reading the previous chapters, it is possible you still cannot definitively decide which "one" spirit type you are. Perhaps, you see yourself fitting several of the spirit descriptions. This is natural because in reality most people are not purely one type. Spirits within people are comprised more like a fruit salad that contains several different types of fruit, with all of the flavors combining to make an even more savory taste. To further this analogy, picture a great big salad bowl, filled with the seven different kinds of fruits just described; they are cut into pieces, each having the flavor, texture, and qualities of the whole fruit from which it came. Now imagine that when each person is born, his/hers spirit is created from one scoop of this spirituality bowl of fruit. It is the fruits that you receive in your scoop that create your final inner spirit. The odds are that you will get a bit of every fruit type in your scoop, but that you will get a higher proportion of some kinds of fruit than others. In other words, I might get more Plum in my scoop, while you get a lot of Apple in yours, and we both might have a high proportion of Orange and Pineapple. Thus, as we develop in life, some tend to be more Plum spirits who need to be loved but also have some Orange that seeks a bit of adventuresome Plum experiences. Others may have a lot of Apple spirit that helps them be precise and correct, but they too may have some Orange that desires some adventures. But they may seek adventures with more of an Apple flavor. The Plum's experiences may be riding roller coasters, while the Apple's may be adventures with investing in the stock market.

The great majority of the people tend to be able to identify one core primary spirit and two secondary ones that very accurately reflect their overall spirit blend. Our unique blend of spirits helps us successfully negotiate the diversity of spirits we likely encounter on a daily basis. Because we have a little of each spirit type within us, we are capable of positively relating to all spirit types. Still each of us should be true to our primary spirit and not neglect its needs.

Neglect may accidentally occur when one's environment is not supportive of the primary spirit or simply because the unique spirit type is not recognized. For example, a Plum growing up in a family environment that has no other Plum members, may not get the love and affection it needs in the way it needs it. The young Plum may need hugs and loving-kindness, but it simply was born into a non-hugging impersonal family. In such a case the Plum will likely adapt by seeking expression of one of its secondary spirit needs as a compensatory coping and survival response. It may strive to be more Apple-like for the Apple dad and succeed in school or move to be more Pineapple-like for the mom and seek approval. This adaptation can occur with any spirit combination. The result usually is lower self-esteem for the child, and stress and frustration for both the parents and children. To the extreme the child's spirit potential may suffer severely or even be lost because its natural primary spirit has not been nourished. When this happens, the individual will develop defenses that can lead to maladaptive behaviors such as depression, anxiety, guilt, or anger. The key to preventing unnecessary defense development is to recognize one's own primary spirit type and those of others and then to meet those spirit specific needs.

To help in the identification of your primary and secondary spirit types, complete the following assessment instrument, *The Spirit Profile Assessment*. And to get a more reliable profile, have one or more people who are close to you also complete this for you too. Sometimes it helps to see our spirit through another's eyes. Talk about the results that you all arrived at and decide upon your primary and secondary spirit blend. This assessment will likely validate your previous working hypothesis about the type of your primary spirit, while also giving you an objective indicator about your likely secondary spirit types. Remember, it is this blended spirit that defines who you are at the core and helps you establish authentic relationships with others.

Spirit Profile Assessment

Each of the following questions is to be answered "true" or "false." Answer the questions in consecutive order and do not skip or omit any of them. Some may seem vague or may not seem to fit your experience: simply choose the answer that first comes to mind when you read the question: mark (✗) in the column under (T) for the statements that you agree with or that are mostly true from your perspective and (F) for those items that you disagree with or are mostly false based on your perspective. Be sure one of the two boxes for each question has a mark in it.

Answer True (T) or False (F) by marking
(✗) in the appropriate box.

	T	F
1. When I hang a picture, I prefer to use a level just to be sure it is straight.	☐	☐
2. I enjoy romantic love story movies.	☐	☐
3. When I am invited out, I would rather the other person decide where we go.	☐	☐
4. I believe that "love at first sight" is possible and even probable.	☐	☐
5. I love taking the risk of driving way above the speed limit.	☐	☐
6. People can get to know others best by simply talking to them.	☐	☐
7. I can do the same thing over and over and never get bored.	☐	☐
8. I rarely find a person that I don't get along with.	☐	☐
9. I prefer my closet to be organized and if possible color-coded.	☐	☐
10. I believe in tough love and give it to everyone I know.	☐	☐
11. I often make a to-do list and then lose it before completing it.	☐	☐
12. I believe in, "try it you'll like it" and even if you don't, you'll have a new experience."	☐	☐
13. I prefer being in groups where I don't stand out.	☐	☐
14. I have no problem giving an hour-long speech on a topic with no prior notice.	☐	☐
15. I love going "where no one has gone before."	☐	☐
16. There are good people and bad people-it is as simple as that.	☐	☐

	T	F
17. You need the right tool for the right job to get the job done right.	☐	☐
18. I frequently have trouble standing up for what I believe.	☐	☐
19. I love to sit and daydream about life's possibilities.	☐	☐
20. I have my smart phone with me, but usually cannot find it quick enough to answer it.	☐	☐
21. I love to travel to collect stories and pictures to share with others.	☐	☐
22. I don't remember the last time I cried and would not tell you if I did.	☐	☐
23. I like to join organizations just to be around others similar to me.	☐	☐
24. The best invention of this century is the computer.	☐	☐
25. My thoughts often tell me one thing and my feelings often tell me the opposite at the same time.	☐	☐
26. Strangers are friends you have not talked with yet.	☐	☐
27. My desk is usually very organized.	☐	☐
28. I pay my bills online using bill pay and have that synched with my computer.	☐	☐
29. I often run a bit late for appointments because I was chatting with someone.	☐	☐
30. I would volunteer to be the first person on a time machine, even if I knew there was a chance it might not work.	☐	☐
31. People often see me as being humble, but I just like to blend in.	☐	☐
32. Education should educate both the mind and the heart.	☐	☐
33. Feelings are more important to me than thoughts.	☐	☐
34. Love is the highest principle that one can live by.	☐	☐
35. "Carpe Diem" (Seize the Day) is one of my favorite values.	☐	☐
36. I feel more comfortable playing the same games with the same people over and over.	☐	☐
37. I must have goals to accomplish in life and create activities that enable me to meet them and I expect to be rewarded when I do.	☐	☐
38. I prefer a mate that will show me their love by doing things to make my life easier.	☐	☐

	T	F

39. I must consider what a person is going to become in life before I can commit to that person. ☐ ☐

40. If I start climbing, I have to go all the way to the top of the mountain. ☐ ☐

41. I actively keep in touch often with as many people from my past as I can. ☐ ☐

42. The best kind of love makes your heart sing each day. ☐ ☐

43. I rarely read the directions to put something together. I know I can do it quicker on my own; besides the people writing them don't really know what they are doing. ☐ ☐

44. I care more about people's feelings than their rights. ☐ ☐

45. I don't just watch people at the airport, I visit with them. ☐ ☐

46. I tend to be naturally quiet and reserved. ☐ ☐

47. Common sense is not so common anymore. ☐ ☐

48. If I can't lead the group then I simply don't want to be a part of it. ☐ ☐

49. Sometimes I get so excited about love that I cannot sleep. ☐ ☐

50. I believe in the idea, don't knock it until you have tried it. ☐ ☐

51. I like saving money by coupon shopping. ☐ ☐

52. There is no such thing as being harsh or blunt, it is just being honest. ☐ ☐

53. Regardless of age, you are never too old to ride a roller coaster. ☐ ☐

54. I have a great collection of stories I love to share with people. ☐ ☐

55. People can't be too sensitive. ☐ ☐

56. If I had to choose between philosophy and technology, I would always choose technology. ☐ ☐

57. I'd rather have someone to talk to more than anything else. ☐ ☐

58. I don't mind doing the little things that most others prefer not to do. ☐ ☐

59. I'd have no problem firing someone from their job; in fact I might like it if it is needed. ☐ ☐

60. I like to have the directions given to me first and then carefully follow them step by step to complete the task the way they want it. ☐ ☐

	T	F
61. I would much more prefer to be in the follower-role than the leader-role.	☐	☐
62. I often push my body to its limit just to see what that limit is.	☐	☐
63. I never question the authority of my superiors and expect my subordinates not to question mine.	☐	☐
64. After an hour or two of sharing people will really know me pretty well.	☐	☐
65. Causalities are an acceptable price for achieving the goal.	☐	☐
66. I often go outside in wild stormy weather to just to experience it.	☐	☐
67. I sometimes cry even when I am happy.	☐	☐
68. I am my own worst critic because I worry about how I am coming across to others.	☐	☐
69. I believe in the saying "when the going gets tough, the tough get going."	☐	☐
70. I am best whenever I follow a carefully worked out plan.	☐	☐

Tally

	PI	A	PL	PE	C	B	O
1. Circle the item number of each true (**T**) response on the scales to the right. Write the number of the true responses per column in the space provided	3	1	2	6	10	7	5
	8	9	4	14	16	13	12
	11	17	19	21	22	18	15
	20	24	33	26	43	23	30
	25	27	34	29	48	31	35
	32	28	42	41	52	36	40
	38	37	44	45	59	46	50
	47	39	49	54	63	58	53
	51	56	55	57	65	60	62
	68	70	67	64	69	61	66

Total circled true items
in each column

☐ ☐ ☐ ☐ ☐ ☐ ☐

Write the Name of your highest 3 score columns in the boxes below

☐

Highest Score Name

☐

2nd Highest Score Name

☐

3rd Highest Score Name

KEY: PI = Pineapple; A = Apple; PL = Plum; PE = Peach; C = Coconut; B = Banana; O = Orange

Your personal fruit blend is your Primary fruit (your Highest Score Spirit name) plus your 2nd and 3rd Highest score names.

Example: Plum (Primary) with some significant Orange (2nd) and Peach (3rd)

Note: In the event of a tie score-ask your friends which one is more evident to them and review the chapter summaries to see which fits best.

You should now have a general profile of your unique human spirit, one primary type and one or two secondary types. Utilizing your answers from your *Spirit Comparison Worksheet*, the descriptive information from the seven Spirit-type chapters and your results from the *Spirit Profile Assessment* should complete your decoding process. You should now have clarity in precisely recognizing your own unique spirit (blend) and also be able to quickly identify spirit types in other people you value. It is now time to turn our attention to the application and use of the deciphered codes.

Chapter 10 provides four simple guidelines for self-care and self-development of your own primary and secondary spirits. Chapter 11 provides a description and model for the four essential pillars for all successful spirit-to-spirit relationships, while chapter 12 concludes by providing ten relationship principles that will help you create long lasting and authentic spirit-based relationships.

SECTION 4

Applying The Fruit Code to Your Relationships

Love is that condition in the human spirit so profound that it empowers us to develop courage; to trust that courage and build bridges with it; to trust those bridges and cross over them so we can attempt to reach each other.

—Maya Angelou

CHAPTER 10

Self Care
To Thine Own SELF Be True

To Thine Own SELF

The acronym SELF with the letters representing the phrase, "Spirit Energy Lasting Forever," was introduced in chapter 1. The idea it signifies is that one's true self is one's inner spirit, an energy system that, if nourished properly, will last beyond our lifetime. Our outside personality is only the "fruit of the spirit," a partial and not always accurate reflection of our spirit and is temporal in nature. It is the development of our unique inner spirit that must be the focal point of attention for us to reach our potential as humans. And it is imperative that this SELF development work be done before we can achieve authentic relationships with others. There are four essential steps to successful SELF development.

> Step One: Correctly identify your spirit type (spirit blend) in order to provide your spirit the correct type of nourishment to maximize its growth.

The entire book to this point has offered you assistance in correctly identifying the spirit type within you. If you still have questions about what kind of spirit you primarily are, reread the Spirit type descriptions, compare your completed *Spirit Comparison Worksheet* to the *Spirit Comparison Worksheets* for each spirit/fruit type, review the spirit **Code Summaries** at the end of each chapter, and be sure to take the *Spirit Profile Assessment* in chapter 9. Ask trusted friends and family who know you if the spirit and spirit blended types you have identified for yourself fit what they see. Once you have clearly identified your spirit blend, you are ready to begin the proper nourishing, maintenance, and fueling processes for your own inner spirit. Remember, we can only give to others what we ourselves possess. So, you must possess an inner spirit with surplus positive energy that allows your spirit light to shine brightly into the world.

Step Two: Be SELF interested; Allot time for
your spirit nourishment each day.

The Bible says, "You shall love your neighbor as yourself" (Mathew 12:31, NET). Often we place so much emphasis on loving others, that we overlook the fact that you must first love yourself fully. We get so busy doing for others that we don't make time for ourselves each day. In spirit terms, you must love your spirit by creating an environment on a daily basis that fills your unique spirit's needs, develops its unique DNA (Distinguishing Notable Attributes), and creates an inner language that will project a clear energetic voice to other spirits. So review the spirit **Code Summary** at the end of the chapter for your primary spirit type and then be sure you are supporting your inner spirit by providing those specific things regularly.

For example, if you are primarily a Plum spirit, make yourself the most juicy (sensitive), tender (caring) Plum spirit anyone can find by being as loving, gentle, and compassionate in your daily life today with yourself as you possibly can. Make yourself the first priority in your daily schedule by setting aside significant time for self-care that is Plum specific. Some of these activities may include, making self-affirmations, being surrounded with feeling oriented people, playing with beloved pets, or watching romantic movies. Take a long leisurely bubble bath as you listen to your favorite love songs. Laugh a little and cry a little to bring your beautiful feelings to the surface each day. Enjoy the fullness of your tender loving spirit today and then tomorrow challenge yourself to be more gentle, loving, sensitive, and compassionate with yourself through another set of Plum activities and people.

Each spirit type has a specific set of needs, a different language, and a unique DNA. Become familiar with your type and then create a SELF care system (activities, people, environments) around those elements each day.

Step 3: Do Not compare yourself to others

Regardless of what kind of spirit you are, loving yourself means to stop comparing yourself to other spirits who are different, not better or worse, just different. As you have read in the earlier chapters of this book, each spirit has wonderful unique abilities, traits, and gifts as well as obstacles to which it is vulnerable. Practice using your unique spirit's special abilities on a daily basis and you will quickly ripen into the special spirit you were intended to be. Most important of all, stop trying to change yourself or others into a type of spirit, neither of you ever was intended to be.

Perhaps, a word of warning is necessary. There remain many pressures in today's world for you not to be yourself and just as many messages not to love yourself. The mass media will tell you to change the color of your hair, encourage you to wear makeup to help you look more "natural" and to hide your unsightly aging spots from others who also have aging spots which they are hiding from you. Men are told to have a six-pack for their abdomen, and muscles so big in their arms that their shirts won't fit. Women are told to wear shoes to make them taller and panties to hide the wrinkles that every behind has. We are all told to wear deodorants to make us smell like pine trees and daffodils rather than human beings. It is tough to be yourself when you smell like a pine tree, are constricted by tight pantyhose, and are in shoes that kill your feet by the end of the day.

It is also difficult to be yourself in schools because you really are never more than a label—slow learner or gifted, "A" student or "B" student. Schools make you learn things that you might not want to remember on an unnatural time schedule. Few students want to learn the life cycle of a pinecone at 7:00 a.m.

And of course, families have good intentions, but unintentionally give the same messages not to be you or love yourself. You may not naturally be a really neat person by nature (like Oranges), but they will love you more if you make your bed which you know you are only going to mess up again that night. And, of course match your socks (like Apples do)—what would people "think" of you (and of them as your parents) if your socks did not match? In reality you are often more loved if you adopt without question more of your family values even if they oppose those of your inner spirit. This is not to criticize families, but we just have not educated families about the immense blessing of having different spirit types from which to learn and for whom to love just as they are.

Every day there are thousands of messages surrounding you throughout our society that others are not happy with you the way you naturally are and that you better change. The good news is that society mostly wants outside changes since for the most part it has not recognized the power of the inner spirit. You will easily recognize these messages when you ripen your inner spirit. When you recognize these messages, say to yourself, "I have to be me at all costs." and I really love my spirit just the way it is. While some less ripe spirits may label you selfish; just think of it as being SELF interested. So start loving yourself by being yourself from the inside out. It is then that you will be in charge of the circumstances of your life, rather than letting the circumstances of your life be in charge of you. If you start each day and end each day with SELF love, some spirits are going to eventually look at you and say—"Wow he or she is the sweetest Plum, the most delicious Pineapple, the freshest Apple, the tastiest Coconut, the juiciest Peach, the best Banana, or the most refreshing Orange I have ever seen in my life and I want them to flavor my life too.

It is only after loving yourself unconditionally and fueling your spirit energy that you will be prepared to have authentic relationships with others.

Step 4: Avoid Toxic People, Activities, and
Environments as much as possible

Steps 1, 2, and 3 emphasized bringing the unique positive elements of your spirit profile (DNA, needs, language, etc.) into your daily life to create a positive environment for your spirit to grow and develop. These are your spirit's healthy nutritional elements. But just like our bodies, we can take in things that are not good or that even might do harm to our spirit. It is just as important to eliminate or minimize the negative elements in our environment, as it is to have the presence the positive elements.

In Step 4 it is important to get a gauge on what is toxic to our spirit and what is healthy A simple test can help you determine whether a particular element in your environment (person or activity) is healthy or not. Before a particular activity or encounter with a person in your life, subjectively rate on a 1 to 10 scale how much energy you currently feel with your inner spirit with 1 representing "no energy" and 10 being "overflowing with positive energy." If you decide that you are a "7" (better than average energy) before the activity or encounter and then are an "8," "9," or "10" after the activity or encounter, this indicates something healthy was transmitted to your spirit. Your spirit was being positively fueled. If however, after the activity or encounter you feel more like a "1, 2, 3, 4, 5, or 6" you need to consider the possibility that the activity or person may not be healthy for your spirit because it drained your spirit of energy. The key is not just a one-time activity or encounter, since anyone may have a bad day and not all activities are always energy producing. But if the same activity or same person is consistently draining, then that likely means that the person and/or activity is life taking to your spirit. Once aware of this consistent pattern of being drained, you need to avoid as much as possible doing the activity or encountering that particular person. Remember your goal is to energize your spirit on a daily basis so maximize positive self-care and minimize toxic ones.

Once you have a SELF care plan permanently in place, one that consistently keeps your spirit energy at an "8" or higher, then you are ready to begin creating the foundation for authentic relationships with other ripe spirits. In other words, now that you love you on a daily basis in action and deeds, you can now love your neighbor successfully.

CHAPTER 11

The Four Pillars of Spirit-Based Relationships and Relationship Actualization

The Four Pillars of Spirit-Based Relationships

There are two types of relationships. One type is created from the outside of one person and connects to the outside of another person. I call these personality-based relationships because they are based on matching outside things like personality, interests, physical appearance, social status, or even practicality between partners. This type of relationship may form quickly and seem ready to last. But in reality, this type has great difficulty enduring long-term as the winds of time, the rains of change, the trials of disappointment and even the triumphs of individual success batter and wear down their shallow surface foundation.

The second type of relationship is formed with the inside of each partner connecting. Specifically, the inner spirit of one partner connects to the inner spirit of the other partner. I call these spirit-based relationships. Because they are built on a deep and permanent foundation comprised of solid relationship building blocks, they successfully weather the winds of time, the rains of change, the trials of disappointment and even the triumphs of success. This is the amazing type of relationship that is timeless in nature.

Usually, when something goes wrong in relationships, it is our personalities or egos that are imposing their defenses, insecurities, and flaws onto our spirits. If we do not have the proper foundation, the relationship, regardless of its nature, will break. The way to avoid this heartbreaking outcome is to begin by building all your relationships on a strong spirit-centered foundation. Such a spirit-centered foundation must incorporate four distinct elements that I call "The Four Pillars for Spirit-based Relationships." These pillars include the following: Openness, Honesty, Trust, and Freedom. Each pillar will be discussed separately. The chapter will conclude with the presentation of an integrated model of "The Four Pillars" that illustrates their dynamic spiritual interaction across time.

The First Pillar: Openness

Openness is the first essential element for spirit-based relationships. By openness, I mean, "to what degree are you willing to share your feelings, thoughts, intentions, beliefs, experiences, etc., with other individuals and at the same time receive others' feelings, thoughts, intentions, beliefs, experiences, etc. back regardless of similarity to yours." It is easy to share things we are sure people similar to us will embrace. But the true test of openness becomes the degree that we are willing to share things that we perceive other individuals are likely not to accept and that may even challenge their beliefs. At the same time, how open are we to different points of view, diverse values, and dissimilar beliefs? It is precisely this willingness to exchange potentially uncomfortable information and make us vulnerable that creates the first foundation pillar for authentic and lasting relationships. While openness in personality-centered relationships may exist on a continuum, ranging from "no openness" to "total openness," spirit-based partners must be completely open with each other. Overall, it is the degree that we can open ourselves up to others, and be open to them (particularly those that are different type spirits than us) that largely determines the potential for both the quality and duration of the relationship itself.

The Second Pillar: Honesty

Honesty is the second mandatory foundation pillar for spirit-based relationships. It can be understood as "the extent to which a person is truthful about his or her feelings, thoughts, intentions, beliefs, experiences, etc." in the relationship. Honesty, like openness may be on a continuum with "perfect honesty" at one end and "complete dishonesty" at the other end of the spectrum in personality-based relationships. However, spirit-based relationships demand complete honesty from both partners. No little white lies are acceptable in true spirit-based relationships; nor are they necessary when openness has been achieved. The extent that we are not honest with another person about who we are or how we perceive them to be is the exact degree to which the relationship potential will be limited in duration and quality and will be worn down over time. Only complete honesty ensures the permanent foundation for a true spirit-based relationship.

The Third Pillar: Trust

Trust is the third essential foundation pillar for spirit-based relationships. It can be defined as "the strength of your conviction in a relationship partner's reliability." Once again, for spirit-based relationships, we need to develop "complete" trust in our partners. Unlike openness and honesty that can be offered immediately to relationships, trust does take time to develop, because it is based on consistency over time in intentions, actions, and responses. A shared past of some duration is necessary to create solid trust in all relationships. But once again, for spirit-based relationships to be actualized to full potential, complete trust needs to be established at some point and be mutual between the two partners. Trust is a precious gift, one that our spirits naturally seek. Once established, it never needs to be questioned again if you have a complete foundation of openness, honesty, trust, and freedom.

The Fourth Pillar: Freedom

Freedom is the final foundation pillar necessary for spirit-based relationships. Freedom in relationships may be defined as "having the ability to act or change without constraint." Freedom means being able to independently make personal choices without judgment or restriction, knowing your partner will support you. Freedom is the hallmark of spirit-based relationships because it encourages partners to be themselves, provides them unconstrained ability to interact with others, supports their freedom to succeed and permits their freedom to fail. What a powerful gift of love this foundation pillar represents. And perhaps even more wonderful is that by giving this gift of freedom to others you are likely to receive an amazing gift back. You will receive the freedom to express your spirit SELF fully, to explore your world independently and interdependently as you choose, and no doubt you will have a committed partner who fully appreciates you for just being you. How sad it is when I see people putting their most cherished relationships into tiny security boxes that they also then have to crawl inside to be with that partner. I encourage you to rip open these boxes containing your relationships, celebrate differences, and share full freedom with all the spirits you value.

The Spiritual Dynamics and Interaction Products of the Four Pillars

Each of the pillars alone represents a powerful relationship construct. But the real magic of this fourfold foundation is how these four elements combine in a spiritual alchemy to create a permanent and timeless foundation for relationship success. The dynamic interaction of these four elements will next be discussed.

Openness and honesty are the first two foundation pillars. While each separately is critical, the blending of the two elements forms the primary connection of "friendship." And more importantly, the merging of openness and honesty gives birth to the presence of the spiritual gift of "hope" in the relationship. Hope is a positive link to the future and as hope permeates the relationship, it signals that the relationship has a healthy and unlimited future. Simply put, once I openly and honestly share who I am with you and you share honestly and openly about yourself, we have created a solid (hopeful) spirit-based foundation upon which to build our future relationship. This could be a permanent friendship, a dynamic sibling/spousal relationship, an engaging mentorship, or any number of robust relationship types. Conversely, lack of openness and/or honesty between two people indicates a more limited personality-based relationship that does not create hope and leads to a more vulnerable relationship over time.

The merging of the second two elements, trust and freedom also gives birth to a spiritual gift between two partners. This gift is "faith." Faith is created in spirit-based partnerships when over time each partner develops an unwavering trust in the other partner's intentions, behaviors, and responses which encourage each to have the total freedom to make independent choices as they interface with the world. Thus, faith is a positive link created over time from past interactions with the partner. There has been a shared history of positive interaction for both partners for some duration of time with the outcome being more "faith" in the permanence and authenticity of the relationship.

The final spiritual gift emerges from the amalgamation of all four pillars. With the presence of relationship "Hope" (future) as a result of the merger of openness and honesty, and relationship "Faith" (past), the product of a positive shared history, the creation of unconditional "Love" (present) becomes the inevitable spirit outcome in each moment.

Illustration 1 gives a visual representation of how "The Four Pillars" interact to create the presence of Hope, Faith, and Love in spirit-based relationships. It also illustrates how each of these is linked temporally to ensure that spirit-based relationships are on a rock hard permanent foundation that spans the relationships' past, present, and future.

The Four Pillars of Spirit-to-Spirit Based Relationships

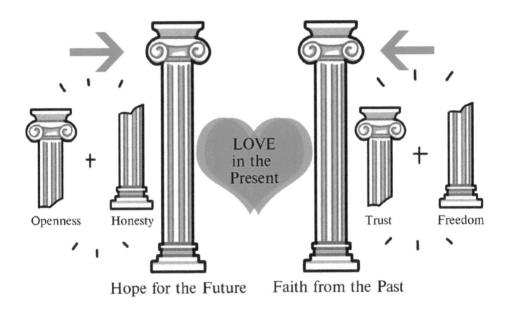

Illustration 1

The Spirit Gifts of the Four Pillars of Spirit-Based Relationships

With the foundation now firmly in place for spirit-based relationships, it is time to present ten guiding principles for creating authentic relationships with other spirit-types.

CHAPTER 12

Love Thy Neighbor
Ten Principles for Spirit-Based
Relationship Success

Love Thy Neighbor: Ten Principles for Spirit-
Based Relationship Success

The French poet, Paul Claudel once wrote,

> Not one of our fellow humans, even if they
> wished, could fail us. In the most unfeeling miser,
> in the innermost being of the prostitute, in the
> foulest drunkard, is an immortal soul intent on
> keeping alive, and which, shut out from the light
> of day, worships in the night. I hear them speak-
> ing when we speak and weeping when I kneel
> and pray. I accept all this! I reach out to them all.
> There is not one that I do not need or that I can-
> not do without. I am my brother's keeper. I dare
> not turn my back on his needs without turning
> my back on my needs as a person. I cannot deny
> him love, without losing it myself.

Everyone has an inner spirit waiting to be noticed and that spirit
has a story from which we can learn. As Claudel so powerful stated,
there is no one that we do not need. If we are indeed our brothers'
and sisters' keepers, we need to learn how to create authentic relationships with others to ultimately serve our creator. This book will
conclude with the presentation of ten relationship principles to help
you apply the information you have learned to create successful spirit-based relationships with all spirit types.

Principle 1: Look closely for the spirit
within others and invite it out.

As discussed in chapter 1, we tend to look at the outside of
people, their appearance, personality, interests, etc., in relationships
before initiating a relationship. In doing so we often miss engaging
wonderful spirits that have much to offer. This first principle sug-

gests a shift from looking to the outside aspects of the other person to looking inside the other as a first relationship step. We do this by looking, engaging, listening, observing, and being present in the moment. Specifically, when you meet a person, look at them and make appropriate eye contact. The English Proverb, "the eyes are the windows of the soul" reflects the importance of this. By glancing into another's eyes we are establishing personal contact with their inner being and are signaling our full attention of creating an authentic connection.

Next we must actively engage the other person's spirit. Give a sincere compliment (you have a great smile or you seem like a special person). Then ask a few personal real questions such as, "What things are going well for you now in your life? What activities uplift you? How did you become so positive?" Then actively listen to the responses. This means not only hearing their words, but also understanding the meaning behind their words. It means listening for the story of the inner spirit by observing their body language (a key cue to recognizing the inner spirit type) as they share to fully understand the meaning of their words. This advanced state of empathy strengthens the spirit connection by paving the way for clear two-way communication.

Most important, be present with the other person. Turn off your phone, ensure you are not interrupted, and focus your attention on the spirit of the person with whom you are interacting, even if it is just for a few minutes. People will be eager to share their inside spirit, if given the invitation.

Principle 2: Identify the spirit type within and
respond to its unique needs (not yours)

Once you have successfully engaged others, then it is time to apply the information you learned in this book to those relationships to determine the other person's type of inner spirit. You have likely already been successful in identifying primary spirit types in family and friends and as you interact with more people, it will be easier to identify specific spirit types more quickly. Remember that the outside personality is only the "fruit of the spirit" and can convey only limited and perhaps even distorted information about the inner spirit type. To fully identify the spirit type of another, watch their non-verbal signals, pay attention to the person's vocabulary, look for consistencies and inconsistencies between their words and behaviors, and notice how they interact with others. For example, Plums tend to use a lot of "touchy-feely" words and mannerisms, while Apples tend to look up with their eyes (toward their brains) when thinking and use the word "think" a lot. Peaches tend to talk with their entire bodies and may even invade your space, while the volume of their voice combined with abrupt short sentences may indicate Coconuts. Pineapples will ask you for your opinion to any question you ask them, while, Oranges will want to do something rather than talk or at least do an activity while talking. Bananas may be in a bunch and just will be assessing you to see how they fit. Be careful not to read too much into the content of the verbal sharing of others. Spirits can be identified by their consistent behaviors. Plums will watch a lot of romantic movies, Apples will spend much time on their computers, Peaches will always be close to or on their smart phones, while Coconuts do activities in which they are in charge. Bananas will volunteer for tasks others don't want to do, while Pineapples will ask what they can do to help you out (and gain your approval). Using the combination of verbal and nonverbal cues with their behavioral counterparts will give you an excellent indicator as to the type of spirit you are engaging.

It also may be helpful to observe closely how other spirits initiate or do not initiate contact. Do they more frequently initiate contact with you and with others (extroverts) or do they wait for you or others to initiate contact with them (introverts)? This will give you an idea of where their spirit energy is focused. Plums, Apples, and Bananas usually focus their energy inward as they process information from the outside world, so you may have to initiate contact with these spirit types. Conversely, Peaches, Coconuts, and Oranges process the world externally and are not shy about making their presence known. They are usually more extroverted and will freely share their feelings and thoughts while also initiating relationship actions without hesitation.

Another dimension to notice when identifying other spirit types is the language they use the most to interface with others. Plums and Peaches interface primarily through feelings; Apples and Coconuts through thoughts; and Bananas and Oranges through actions. In other words, Plums and Peaches are feelers; Apples and Coconuts are thinkers; and Bananas and Oranges are doers. Illustration 2 provides a useful summary that illustrates spirit type by preferred language interface and energy focus. Notice, that Pineapples are the in-between spirit on all dimensions. They are a little bit of feeler, thinker, and doer and may change this preference at any moment. They also vacillate between being introverted and extroverted depending on the situation and person they are experiencing. Thus, if you have difficulty in recognizing a particular energy flow direction or observe differing language interfaces from the same person, that person probably has a Pineapple spirit.

SPIRIT TYPE by
LANGUAGE INTERFACE & ENERGY FOCUS
PRIMARY LANGUAGE INTERFACE

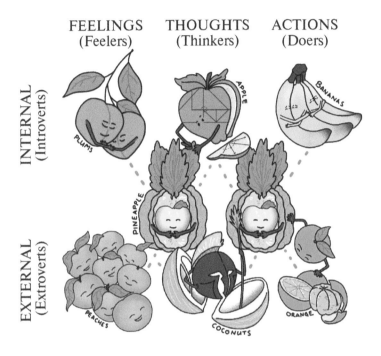

| FEELINGS (Feelers) | THOUGHTS (Thinkers) | ACTIONS (Doers) |

INTERNAL (Introverts)

EXTERNAL (Extroverts)

ENERGY FOCUS

Illustration 2

One last tip in accurately identifying spirit types of others is that you should pay closer attention to how the other spirit is interacting with other people than yourself. You are likely to get a more accurate indication of the type of spirit by watching interactions with others than interactions with yourself because you will be more objective in your observations than when you are immersed in the relationship itself. Thus, if the person volunteers their services widely, Bananas are present; if they take control in multiple venues, Coconuts are likely. If they are always precise to a fault, the Apple spirit is likely and so forth. Consistency of behaviors usually indicates the satisfying of one's primary spirit needs.

Finally, it is always fun to simply have them complete the *Spirit Profile Assessment*, but be careful, Coconuts may be offended; Apples will think it is not valid; Peaches will rather talk than write; Pineapples will do it to please; Bananas will do it if everyone else does, and the Plums will enjoy the feeling the assessment brings. Oranges will likely make a paper airplane out of it and fly the plane.

Be sure to identify the primary spirit type of the people with whom you desire authentic relationships.

Principle 3: Ensure that the Spirits you
seek in relationships are "ripe."

It is critical to your success in all relationships, regardless of the particular spirit with which you are interacting, that it be optimally ripe, not under or over ripe. If it is not yet ripe, it will not know itself fully and may quickly change directions in the relationship without warning. Relationships with unripe spirits are usually very rocky, unstable, unpredictable, and often lead to abrupt painful endings that can jeopardize (bruise) the ripe spirit's self-esteem.

A second and even more serious problem occurs when in relationship with an over-ripe spirit. These spirits may start to rot and rotting is highly contagious. The rotten spirit regardless of variety will bring its rottenness to the relationship. Over-ripe spirits usually pressure others constantly, complain persistently, and are consistently negative in their outlook on life and people. They are generally inflexible and resist change, particularly in themselves. It has been said that misery loves company, and so these over-ripe spirits are in constant search of company. It is imperative to stay as far from these over-ripe/rotten spirits as possible. You cannot and must not try to change or rescue these spirits because all that can happen is for you to become infected with their rotten disposition, negative attitudes, and decaying behaviors. I always cite the following example. If you put a healthy piece of fruit and a rotten piece of fruit into the same paper bag, and close it for a few days; when opened, the good piece of fruit does not make the rotten piece of fruit healthy. Rather over time the rotten piece of fruit makes the healthy piece of fruit rotten too. This is exactly what I have observed about people from my counseling perspective. I have watched young children say that they never want to be negative like their parents and after constantly spending time with those parents, I eventually see the children acting exactly like the negative parents. Remember in chapter 11, it was emphasized that if you have people like this in your present life that you find positive ways of eliminating them from your close proximity or your own spirit will be contaminated. For example, if they call you to complain about someone or something, politely disagree and let them know that you will not support their negativity; hang up consistently when the negativity is present. Conversely, if the usually negative individual is unexpectedly positive, reinforce the healthy behavior by pointing out how good it is to talk to a positive person when they are being positive in their behavior. By doing this you will be valuing yourself and also will be forcing others to be positive in relationship to you. These spirits will be forced to either stay positive with you or to find someone else with whom to be negative, which is usually what they do. If there is someone in your life now who is an over-ripe/rotten spirit, they must independently or with the help of a professional excise the rotten part or you must cut him/her out of your close proximity in the described manner before they infect you. You can still love them from afar and pray for them, but be careful being in close contact.

You now may be wondering how to recognize a healthy ripe spirit when you encounter it. Basically, a healthy ripe spirit will be positive in attitude, have good self-esteem, know and appropriately voice its own needs, and is flexible and accepting of others' needs as being different from its own needs. Most importantly, ripe spirits give off energy ("Let your light so shine..." [Mathew 5:16, KJV]), while unripe and over-ripe/rotten ones drain you and take energy away from you. The scaling tool from chapter 10 can help you determine whether a spirit is healthy or not. Before an encounter, subjectively rate on a 1 to 10 scale how much energy you feel within yourself, with one representing "no energy" and 10 being "overflowing with energy." If you decide that you are a "7" (better than average energy) before the encounter and are an "8," "9," or "10" after the encounter you can be pretty sure that you are with a healthy ripe spirit. If however, after the encounter you feel like a "1, 2, 3, 4, 5, or 6" you need to consider the possibility that the other person may not be a healthy ripe spirit and actually may be a life-taker to your spirit. Again, the key is not just in one encounter, since anyone may have a bad day and influence you in a negative way. But unripe and rotten spirits will almost always drain you a little in each encounter and may drain you a lot. Thus, if being with another person frequently drains you, it is likely that they are not a healthy ripe spirit and it is important for you to stay away. It does always take two ripe spirits to succeed in a relationship.

Principle 4: Nourish each ripe spirit type by
meeting its requisite primary needs.

The ultimate success secret of *The Fruit Code: The spiritual shortcut to loving your SELF and others* is contained in this principle. By meeting the inner needs of the spirit with whom you are relating, you will not only jumpstart the relationship, but you will be ensuring future interactions are positive and growth producing. Spirits need to be filled with the right kind of fuel and will naturally seek out those who provide this precisely and regularly for them. Plums will respond to your hugs, Pineapples to your appreciation, Apples to your acknowledgement of their correctness, Peaches to your listening, Coconuts to your loyalty, Bananas to your support and Oranges to the freedom you provide them to experience life. Give each spirit type what it needs and if you have identified the spirit correctly, the relationship will flourish.

Remember to adhere to "The Four Pillars for Spirit-Based Relationships."

1. Be open to different types and embrace the wonderful diversity of spirits
2. Be honest with others about your needs
3. Trust yourself and others in the relationship over time
4. Give others the freedom to totally be themselves

Using the four pillars and meeting the exact spirit type need regularly for others will create a powerful spirit-based relationship.

Principle 5: Spend quality time with each
significant spirit in your life.

On first glance, this activity may seem obvious, but sociologists tell us that this is not happening in families or even in most marriages. And these are relationships in which we would expect the most quality time to be spent. Spirit-based relationships cannot grow to their full potential without quality time being spent between relationship partners on a regular basis. So what is quality time?

Quality time is time spent between any two individuals in which both partners give the other undivided attention without any external noise (television, children, etc.), functional activities (cleaning the house, washing the car, etc.) that create distractions, or interruptions (phone calls or messages from others) of that time between the two individuals. Quality time should always increase the feelings of closeness between the two partners and may be expressed physically, emotionally, verbally, or even recreationally. For optimum spirit growth, I encourage always seeking a balance between the physical, emotional, and intellectual components of quality time.

This fifth principle is critical because all of the initial steps (looking inwardly for spirits, correctly identifying and meeting the specific type needs of those spirits, ensuring ripeness in other spirits, as well as promoting openness, honesty, trust, and freedom) are useless unless there is regular time free from distractions for your relationship partners. The relationship will suffer without sufficient quality time and the reason is quite simple. Because both spirits and relationships are dynamic in nature and are ever changing and growing, they need frequent quality contact in order to understand and adapt to the changes taking place within each individual. Thus, it is imperative to spend quality time regularly with those individuals who are important to you. The more important they are, the more quality time needs to be spent. How often I have seen couples breaking up because one partner has gone off to school, while the other has tended home. Upon the return from school, they are unable to adjust. Both say the other has changed and they are now attempting to bridge a wide communication gap that should never have risen. Quality time ensures that you are growing together in your relationship. If this time is not spent, then you will grow apart. Choose to grow together rather than apart by spending quality time with those spirits you value.

There is another reason for spending this quality time with your spirit-based partners. The most precious commodity you possess is not the air you breathe, the food you eat, or the water you drink. After you are long gone from this earth, there will still be plenty of air, food, and water. The most precious commodity you have because of its scarcity and its irreplaceable value is your time. Even the longest of lives is but a mere split second in eternity. Thus, your time is precious. When you choose to share your time in quality communication with another individual, you are giving that person your most precious spirit gift and that person in turn is giving the same gift back to you. Thus, a special spirit bond is forged when we choose to share our most valued possession, our time, with another person regularly.

You may now be wondering just how much time I am speaking about. Of course this varies with each spirit-based relationship and the nature of that relationship. Again, remember the more valued the relationship to you, the more quality time you should be spending with that person. For personal intimate relationships, such as a marriage, I recommend a minimum of one hour of quality time per day. It may be spent just holding each other, praying together, having coffee in the morning, talking about the events of each other's days, or just sharing feelings in a warm bath. Couples may struggle at first to find this time, but for healthy spirit-based relationships, soon their days will become planned around it.

For less intimate relationships, such as employer to employee or even neighbor to neighbor, one hour of quality time every week or two usually will suffice. Friendships fall somewhere in between these two poles. If for some reason it is not physically possible to get together with one's valued relationships, a quality (not newsy) letter or phone call will work almost as well. But be careful of texting—this usually is not quality time. Most important, try to get together in person as often as possible and then spend quality exchange time with those people you value.

While the principle of quality time is intended to apply to any combination of spirit-type relationships, a special word on this principle is needed about same, similar, and opposite spirit relationships. The more different the type of spirit in the relationship from your primary type, the more important quality time becomes to the success of that relationship. It has previously been stated that opposite spirits (Plum/Apple; Banana/Orange; Peach/Coconut, etc.) have to work harder to achieve authentic deep and lasting relationships than same or similar spirits do. Therefore, quality time is essential for understanding differences and meeting the varied needs of each partner. In other words two Plums in relationship to each other may not need as much quality time as an Apple and a Plum in relationship to each other. It is also possible that two Plums can afford not to be as consistent in spending quality time as an Apple and a Plum couple might need. Opposite and more dissimilar spirits simply grow apart more quickly than similar and identical spirits without quality time. Thus, the communication of quality time becomes more essential with the greater the difference in primary spirit types between the two partners. Remember, all spirits either grow together in relationships or apart, and it is the quality time spent on a consistent basis that determines the direction of the growth. It is your choice!

Principle 6: Be positive, think positive,
act positive in all relationships.

There is no greater magnet to attract all spirits than the quality of being positive. Many books have been written on the power of being positive; and this is particularly true for spirit-based relationships. Positive actions, behavior, and attitudes beget positive responses. Being positive demonstrates your ripeness to other spirits and serves as a powerful invitation to others to get to know the spirit within you. Conversely, negative behavior or attitudes will beget negative responses, and a negative attitude will push healthy ripe spirits away from you; you then will be left with mostly unripe and rotten spirits.

It continues to amaze me how few people have learned this skill of being positive or at least how seldom they choose to use it. So many people focus on what is wrong, what is missing, and how unlucky they are. It then becomes a habit and is contagious. I'm reminded of an event that occurs every year on a university campus that I once taught at that illustrates this choice perfectly. In the fall, gorgeous blackbirds start migrating and they choose the beautiful Live Oak trees on the campus as a nightly roost. They fly in by the thousands around sunset; it is an incredible sight to behold; art in motion as they fly and soar and provide a symphony of life sounds to the ear. When the sun was setting those black silhouettes against the orange and pink sky always brought tears of awe to my eyes. I loved seeing them nightly, as did many others. But, there was another large contingent of people who were busy being negative; complaining about the sound and looking down at the bird droppings on the ground, all the while missing nature's aerial splendor. In fact they went so far as to petition the university to have the beautiful trees cut down in order to eliminate the roosts for birds. What a great illustration for life and our relationship to it. Being positive is a choice—you can look up, smile, and enjoy life's magic, or you can look down at the droppings and be disgusted. Just remember, you will attract the kind of spirit that you are yourself. We only have limited time in this world; let your spirit soar by being positive, spending time with positive people, and adding the artistic soaring of another positive spirit to this beautiful world.

Principle 7: Regularly evaluate the fruit
that your relationships produce.

Thus far, all the principles have been concerned with the creation of long lasting authentic spirit-based relationships. Principle 7 is an evaluation step to see how your relationships are progressing. This monitoring step is necessary to ensure that your spirit-based relationships remain healthy. Just like a yearly physical exam checks the body for early signs of physical problems, so this step checks for early signs of relationship issues. A spirit is only as healthy as his or her relationship life, and if not checked periodically, even spirit-based relationships can become unhealthy.

Specifically, in checking your relationships there are several areas with which to be concerned. First, ask yourself, "Is this relationship producing positive energy for both partners or has it become draining to one or both partners?" There will be times when each partner will perhaps, feel drained by the other, but these times should be short in duration and infrequent in occurrence. Energy draining simply means that you do not look forward to being with that person or you might even avoid or find excuses for not getting together with that spirit. Or after getting together with the person, you might find yourself tired, negative, or having a bad attitude. In reviewing each of your valued relationships, if you find any of them to be more energy draining than energy producing over time, then that relationship is certainly in need of help. When you discover that being with a particular relationship partner becomes draining, carefully inspect the nature of that drain and make certain it is only for the moment and does not become a lasting part of the relationship. Remember, healthy spirit relationships more often than not produce positive spirit energy and mutually fuel both partners. This first inspection will tell you much about the health of your relationship. In fact, the more energy you and your relationship partner generate between each other, the healthier the relationship is. But remember it must be mutual and this can only be discovered through quality time and communication.

The second check point is to determine what qualitative effect, other than energy, you are having on others, as well as what effect they are having on you. Are you a more independent, positive, and personally resourceful individual because of your relationship? Or are you more dependent, negative and weak because of your relationship? With the best of intentions, some giving spirits may actually help create a weaker individual. For example, the parent who with good intentions provides for every desire of his or her child, may accidentally spoil the child and cause that child to grow into a weak, negative, selfish, and dependent adult, even though the parent was acting out of what he/she perceived to be love. In terms of relationships, a good rule of thumb is to provide for your relationship partners' needs, but let them satisfy their own desires. This will work in all relationships and is a preventive measure that will promote relationships health. We can only grow together in relationships to the degree that we are growing individually and if we are not growing individually, eventually the relationships important to us will grow apart from us. All healthy spirit-centered relationships should foster personal growth.

A final important relationship health check to conduct is concerned with Principle 5: Quality time. Since this is so critical for communication, check regularly to make certain you are continuing to spend the same quantity of quality time that led initially to the healthy spirit-based relationship. A relationship cannot grow without this time and one of the first telltale signs of a faltering relationship is when this quality time is no longer set aside by one or both partners with the same frequency and for the same duration that was initially provided. If the relationship is important to both partners, they will eagerly provide this quality time. Remember, you will either grow together or apart. There is no middle ground. Thus, in inspecting the health of all relationships, be sure that the quality time remains at the same level or even increases in deepening relationships. There are many distractions in our society that compete for this relationship time, and it is easy to let other things take priority. If you notice any significant decrease in the quality time you spend in any of your particular relationships, point it out to that partner and get it back quickly. The relationship will respond to that quality time being spent and again larger problems may actually be prevented.

Thus, evaluate the health of your relationships periodically. Assess whether they are mutually producing energy. Analyze whether both partners in the relationship are individually more positive, and still personally growing. Finally, ensure that the quality time continues to be spent not only maintaining the relationship, but also to promote its growth and development. If you do all three of these tests regularly, you will ensure that your spirit-centered relationships are indeed healthy and nourishing to both partners.

Principle 8: Be unconditional in your love!

This may be one of the most difficult of all principles to enact. Yet without a doubt it is critical for promoting the success of your relationships and the ripening of your own spirit. It really is not difficult to love or accept another person who sees the world from our own frame of reference or in other words has the same spirit type as us. However, the true test of love is positive acceptance of spirit types that have different expressions of feelings, thoughts, actions, or beliefs than our own. It is all too common for people in the face of differences to try to change themselves or others so that they will feel more comfortable. However, unconditional love means, "I love you just the way you are and I will not ask you to change just to make me feel more comfortable." With unconditional love, there is nothing that others can do to add to our love or to diminish it. Their thoughts, feelings, actions, and beliefs are independent of our love for them. This should be the goal for all spirit-based relationships. It is ironic that so often the more important and intimate the relationship, the less we give it our highest (unconditional) love. How often have we heard adults quickly defend a stranger by saying, "He has a right to his opinion" and then turn to their spouse or children and say "as long as you live with me you will live by my rules." Perhaps, parenting is where we struggle the most to give unconditional love. How often are children convinced by years of conformity and fear of losing their parent's approval, that their parents will no longer love them if they begin acting on their own values, thoughts, feelings, and beliefs. Of course, children are just as likely to put conditions on their love for their parents.

These examples point out how important it is to sow the seeds of unconditional love early in relationships. Practice separating behaviors, thoughts, feelings, and beliefs from your love and acceptance of your relationship partners. Child psychologists have long instructed parents to say to a child, "I love you, but do not approve of those particular actions." Love the person, not the behaviors. From a Christian perspective, love the sinner, not the sin. Feel free to disagree, but do it with loving-kindness. Lead with your spirit's feelings, thoughts, and beliefs so that others will clearly and consistently see who you are. Let those actions be your invitation for others to follow in your path, but never demand that they do as you do or believe as you believe. Lovingly encourage success and the best in others, but reward the honest attempt, not the outcome. A person who does his/her best and earns an "A" grade is no better than a person who does his/her best and earns an "F." Love the effort and the intentions. I'm reminded of a heart-warming memory that reflects unconditional love. I was working in a state hospital for severely developmentally delayed children and adults who were playing a basketball game. These beautiful spirits would run up and down the court laughing and playing and never scored a single point; they were simply enjoying the game. After it was over everyone hugged. I believe that they were God's basketball champions because they gave their best, enjoyed what they were doing, promoted loving relationships, and placed no conditions on themselves or others. Love for anything or anyone to truly be love, must be unconditional. Every time we add a condition to our love for ourselves or for others, we are removing a portion of love equal to that condition. In other words, the more conditions, the less love.

Thus, practice with yourself and all others, unconditional love. It will take work, but the results are amazing. Unconditional love will allow your children and parents to become your friends, your friends to become your brothers and sisters, with the sum total of all your various relationships becoming your one permanent spiritual family.

Principle 9: Always forgive.

Forgiveness is a most powerful spiritual gift. We can know ourselves and seek out others with gifts of openness, honesty, trust, and freedom. We can be as positive as possible and give unconditional love in our quality time with others. We can evaluate our relationships to ensure the fruit is healthy and nourishing, but if we have not learned to forgive, then all of the previous principles will crumble and we will be buried alive by the rubble of failed relationships.

The reason for the importance of this principle is simple, perhaps even self-evident. People are not perfect and cannot be expected to be perfect. Even the ripest of spirits have bruises, spots, or minor defects, and will slip from time to time in their relationships and act less than perfect. The fact of our imperfection is the very glue that holds relationships together. I am never going to be perfect and neither are you so let's do our best, but always remember that we are imperfect. Perhaps, this is the foundation of love that God provides to His imperfect children. Forgiveness is the ultimate gift, for spirit-based relationships.

Forgiving should not be very difficult to do. It is easy to forgive others their flaws when you are truly aware of your own flaws. When there is a mistake made or a hurtful deed done, simply remember how wonderful it was to be forgiven. Start relationships by building forgiveness into them in their early stages, knowing that someday the other person may hurt you and that you may just as easily hurt them because of your own imperfections. When that day comes you will still feel a bit of hurt, but will be ready to forgive. Let your positive thinking and feeling spirit overwhelm the mistakes. Realize because you are in relationship with the other person, you may be partly responsible for the good that is done or for the errors that are made by that individual. This is the nature of relationships. Forgiveness is healing and will lead to riper spirits for both the forgiver and the forgiven with the relationship itself being stronger than it was before the event.

One final note should be added to this discussion. Many people seem to be able to forgive others, but not themselves for their imperfections and mistakes. Be gentle with yourself and realize you are going to make mistakes. Never intentionally hurt others or do wrong, but when it happens, forgive yourself and get yourself going again quickly. Acknowledge that you made a mistake and will learn from that mistake and attempt to never make that exact same mistake again. Learn from your mistakes; they are powerful teachers; then forgive yourself for making them. The most important relationship you have is with yourself, so practice with yourself what you will give and want to receive from others. Forgiveness is indeed a most special spiritual gift for all.

Principle 10: Keep God in the center of
your spirit-based relationships.

The Bible says, "Where two or more are gathered in my name, there am I am among them" (Mathew 18:20, NAS). God needs to be in the center of all valued spirit-based relationships. This concept is so essential to spirit-based relationships that I saved it for last. There must be three spirits in true spirit-based relationship: your spirit, your relationship partner's spirit, and God's spirit, whatever you conceive this to be. It is God that breathes new life into relationships that seem broken; it is God that allows our dreams with others to come true; it is God that compensates and forgives us for our imperfections, and it is in final analysis God to whom our spirits are eternally entrusted. And it was God who placed our spirit and created its particular blend within us. Thus, God must be the center of all spirit-based relationships. Find some path with your spirit partners to invite God to be in the center of your relationship. This may be a formal or informal invitation, but ripe spirits will be welcoming an old friend when they welcome God to the center of the relationship. This mutual invitation will help you fulfill the previous nine principles and ensure the permanence of your spirit-based relationships across time, while filling your days in this earthly domain with diverse, ripe, abundant, and juicy spiritual fruit.

Summary

In summary, there are ten principles that will help produce successful spirit-based relationships with others.

Principle 1: Look closely for the spirit within others and invite it out.
Principle 2: Identify the spirit type within and respond to its particular needs (not yours).
Principle3: Ensure that the spirits you seek in relationships are ripe.
Principle 4: Nourish each ripe spirit type by meeting its requisite primary needs.
Principle 5: Spend quality time with each significant spirit in your life.
Principle 6: Be positive, think positive, act positive in all relationships.
Principle 7: Regularly evaluate the fruit that your relationships produce.
Principle 8: Be unconditional in your love!
Principle 9: Always forgive.
Principle 10: Keep God in the center of your spirit-based relationships.

By following these simple but crucial principles, you will create authentic relationships that in turn will bear very special spiritual fruits. Remember, that you are unlikely to succeed with everyone. Someone may be allergic to your type of spirit. If you fail with one person, go out and try with another. You will succeed more often than you will fail and soon you will have authentic relationships that bear permanent and remarkable fruit for the world to savor!

The fruit of the Spirit is love, joy, peace, patience, kindness, goodness, faithfulness, gentleness, self-control.
—Galatians 5:22-23 RSV

ABOUT THE AUTHOR

Dr. Jeffrey Ickes has been a professor in psychology and counseling for over forty years. He is interested in bridging the gap between applied psychology and religion through teaching people spirit-based skills that will raise their self-esteem, enhance their relationships, and create lasting authentic happiness.